WORKBOOK
with Digital Pack

4

CEFR
B2

TH!NK
SECOND EDITION

Herbert Puchta,
Jeff Stranks &
Peter Lewis-Jones
with Clare Kennedy

CAMBRIDGE
UNIVERSITY PRESS

ACKNOWLEDGEMENTS

Acknowledgements

The authors and publishers acknowledge the following sources of copyright material and are grateful for the permissions granted. While every effort has been made, it has not always been possible to identify the sources of all the material used, or to trace all copyright holders. If any omissions are brought to our notice, we will be happy to include the appropriate acknowledgements on reprinting and in the next update to the digital edition, as applicable.

Keys: UW = Unit Welcome; U = Unit.

Text

U1: National Geographic Creative for the text adapted from 'Instants: Dispatches from the Dawn Wall' by Mallory Benedict & 'Duo Completes First Free Climb of Yosemite's Dawn Wall, Making History' by Andrew Bisharat. Copyright © 2015 National Geographic Creative. Reproduced with permission; **U2**: Text about Réka Kaponay. Reproduced with permission of Réka Kaponay; Text about Cameron Davis. Reproduced with permission of Heather Greenwood Davis; **U9**: St. Martin's Press and Josh Shipp for the text adapted from The Teen's Guide to World Domination: Advice on Life, Liberty, and the Pursuit of Awesomeness by Josh Shipp. Copyright © 2010 St. Martin's Press. Reproduced with permission of Macmillan and Josh Shipp; **U12**: Text adapted from 'Urban Exploration Photographer Finds a Stash of Cash in an Abandoned House' by Michael Zhang. Copyright © PetaPixel; Text adapted from '13 of history's greatest polar explorers' by Laura Moss, http://www.mnn.com/earth-matt ers/animals/photos/13-of-historysgreatest-polar-explorers/ann-bancroft. Copyright © Narrative Content Group.

Photography

The following photographs are sourced from Getty Images.

UW: haoliang/E+; SDI Productions/E+; Maskot/DigitalVision; AzmanJaka/E+; Star Tribune via Getty Images; Thomas Barwick/DigitalVision; **U1**: josefkubes/iStock/Getty Images Plus; Photo and Co/The Image Bank; Jiri Hrebicek/iStock/Getty Images Plus; Zinkevych/iStock/Getty Images Plus; Tetra Images; davidf/iStock/Getty Images Plus; Cavan Images; Comic Relief/Getty Images Entertainment; **U2**: SOPA Images/LightRocket; Education Images/Universal Images Group; Tuul & Bruno Morandi/The Image Bank Unreleased; Gabe Ginsberg/Moment; Grant Finley/EyeEm; **U3**: AlexLMX/iStock/Getty Images Plus; Vyacheslav Prokofyev/TASS; Ababsolutum/E+; denozy/iStock/Getty Images Plus; STEVE HORRELL/SPL/Science Photo Library; SolStock/iStock/E+; paylessimages/iStock/Getty Images Plus; JGI/Jamie Grill; Westend61; SolStock/E+; Prapass Pulsub/Moment; **U4**: Catherine Ledner/Stone; Fred Stein Archive/Archive Photos; monkeybusinessimages/iStock/Getty Images Plus; kutaytanir/E+; **U5**: JordiStock/iStock/Getty Images Plus; Jumpstart Studios/Stone; Gerald Corsi/E+; **U6**: SolStock/E+; **U7**: Greg Hinsdale/The Image Bank; Siriporn Wongmanee/EyeEm; Sol de Zuasnabar Brebbia/Moment; **U8**: Dave J Hogan/Getty Images Entertainment; Pierre-Yves Babelon/Moment; MmeEmil/E+; StephanHoerold/E+; Chakrapong Worathat/EyeEm; duckycards/E+; Anat Chantrakool/EyeEm; Peter Dazeley/The Image Bank; Xacto/E+; **U9**: cokada/E+; LeoPatrizi/E+; T3 Magazine/Future; bbostjan/iStock/Getty Images Plus; What Hi-Fi Magazine/Future; **U10**: Charday Penn/E+; Bettmann; skynesher/E+; **U11**: Space Frontiers/Archive Photos; Anton Petrus/Moment Open; **U12**: Ze Martinusso/Moment; Jacobs Stock Photography Ltd/DigitalVision; SOPA Images/LightRocket; CathWalter/iStock/Getty Images Plus; Star Tribune via Getty Images; Gavriil Grigorov/TASS; Kelly Cheng/Moment; neirfy/iStock/Getty Images Plus; Reuber Duarte/iStock/Getty Images Plus.

The following photographs are sourced from other sources/libraries.

U2: © Cameron Davis; © Réka Kaponay; **U3**: Valery Sidelnykov/Shutterstock; **U11**: AF archive/Alamy Stock Photo.

Cover photography by Francesco Carta fotografo/Moment/Getty Images; Jorg Greuel/Stone/Getty Images.

Illustrations

UW: Ben Scruton; Martin Sanders; **U2**: Pablo Gallego; **U3**: Martin Sanders; Ben Scruton; **U4**: Pablo Gallego; **U5**: Martin Sanders; **U6**: Ben Scruton; **U7**: Pablo Gallego; **U8**: Ben Scruton; **U9**: Pablo Gallego; **U11**: Ben Scruton; **U12**: Pablo Gallego; Martin Sanders.

Video stills

Grammar Rap Video Stills production by Silversun Media Group.

Audio production by Sonica Studios Limited.

CONTENTS

WELCOME

A WHAT A STORY!
Descriptive verbs

1 Circle the correct options.

1 The hurricane *demolished / fled / raged* everything in its path.
2 The surfer *struck / smashed / dived* under the water to escape the boat.
3 The people *smashed / fled / struck* from the hurricane.
4 As she started to fall I managed to *grab / rage / scream* her by the arm.
5 The fire *demolished / raged / dived* through the trees.
6 The people *screamed / grabbed / demolished* in terror as the wave came towards them.
7 The rescuers *smashed / flew / screamed* down a wall to rescue the family.
8 The car was *grabbed / dived / struck* by the falling tree.

Phrasal verbs

2 Complete the sentences. Choose the correct verbs and write them in the correct form.

> break | carry | end | give
> look | sort | stand | take

1 I think I might _____ up yoga. It's really good for body and mind.
2 He studied medicine at university. How _____ he _____ up as an accountant?
3 Can you believe it? Our car_____ down five kilometres from home.
4 I know I should _____ up eating so much chocolate but I think I'd find it too difficult.
5 They_____ on eating their picnic even though it started to rain.
6 When I have a problem my mum always helps me _____ it out.
7 I'm really _____ forward to the summer holidays. No more exams!
8 Billy really _____ out in the class photo because he's so tall.

Elements of a story

3 Match the words with the definitions.

1 hero ☐
2 plot ☐
3 dialogue ☐
4 characters ☐
5 ending ☐
6 opening ☐
7 villain ☐
8 setting ☐

a the people in the story
b a bad man or woman
c how the story starts
d how the story finishes
e the man or woman in the story we identify with
f the place where the story happens
g what the people in the story say
h the storyline

4 Complete the text with the missing words.

So what do you need to write a successful story? Well to start with you need a good
[1] _____ – without a great story you've got no chance. Of course any good story needs a selection of different [2]_____ , a [3]_____ for the reader to identify with and a [4]_____ to hate. And to help bring all these people alive you'll need to have good [5]_____ between them. What they say and how they say it is so important. Then you'll need a [6]_____ for your story. Where and when does the action happen? Is it the modern day, in the past or even in the future?
So now you've got all that, it's time to start writing. The [7]_____ is essential. You'll need to get your reader's attention from the very beginning. And once you've got their attention hopefully, they'll read right through so you'll need to give them a good [8]_____ , too, to make sure they won't feel they've wasted their time.
And that's all you need. That and a lot of luck.

Talking about past routines

5 🔊 W.01 **Listen and put the pictures in order.**

6 **Complete the sentences so that they are true for you.**

1 When I was really young my mum/dad would

_____

2 My first teacher at school used to

_____

3 When I was upset, I used to

_____

4 When it was my birthday, my parents would

_____

5 During the school holidays, I would

_____

SUMMING UP

7 **Put the sentences in order to make a dialogue.**

☐ **Ana** Well, for example, he'd tell a story about how the wind was getting stronger and how we needed to put all the furniture in the cupboard under the stairs. And he'd do all the actions.

1 **Ana** My dad used to tell me really great stories when I was a kid.

☐ **Ana** Really dramatic and exciting stories, and he would pretend they were happening to us.

☐ **Ana** He was. I used to really look forward to his stories. But he gave up telling them as I got older.

☐ **Jake** That's a shame.

☐ **Jake** What kind of stories?

☐ **Jake** He sounds like a really fun dad.

☐ **Jake** What do you mean?

B AN UNCERTAIN FUTURE
Future plans

1 **Match the parts of the sentences.**

1 I don't leave ☐

2 You'll need to get a ☐

3 Many young people are waiting longer to start ☐

4 Before I start my career, I'd love to travel ☐

5 Would you like to make enough money so you can ☐

6 I don't want to settle ☐

a a career these days.

b the world for a year or so.

c retire before you're 60?

d down yet. I'm not ready.

e school for another two years.

f degree in engineering if you want build bridges.

Life plans

2 **Put the events in the order that they happened.**

☐ So I returned home and started doing a degree.

☐ So I decided to travel the world for a while until I made up my mind.

☐ When I was in Asia I suddenly realised what career I wanted to do – teaching.

☐ We started a family after I had been teaching for a few years.

☐ When I left school I wasn't too sure what I wanted to do.

☐ Next year I'm going to retire. I can't help wondering how it all passed so quickly.

☐ After the birth of my second son, I got promoted. I'm now a head teacher.

☐ In my final year of university, I met the love of my life and we settled down.

Future continuous

3 **Complete the sentences. Use the future continuous form of the verbs.**

Two months from now …

1 I _____ on a sunny beach in Greece. (lie)

2 I _____ exams any more. (not do)

3 I _____ delicious food every night. (eat)

4 I _____ every morning at 6 am! (not get up)

5 I _____ in a five-star hotel. (stay)

6 I _____ the bus to school every morning. (not take)

I can't wait for the summer holidays!

Being emphatic: *so* and *such*

4 **Choose the correct options.**

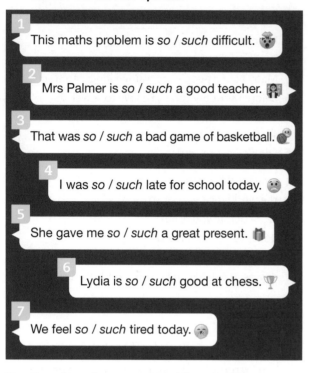

1 This maths problem is *so* / *such* difficult. 🐶

2 Mrs Palmer is *so* / *such* a good teacher. 👩‍🏫

3 That was *so* / *such* a bad game of basketball. 🏀

4 I was *so* / *such* late for school today. 😟

5 She gave me *so* / *such* a great present. 🎁

6 Lydia is *so* / *such* good at chess. 🏆

7 We feel *so* / *such* tired today. 😴

5 **Complete the sentences with *so* or *such*. Then match the sentences with the photos.**

1 It's _____ a clever dog.

2 They're _____ a talented band.

3 I'm _____ excited. I'm going on holiday tomorrow.

4 It's _____ cold today.

5 They're _____ a good team.

6 This pasta is _____ delicious.

Extreme adjectives

6 **Complete the missing adjectives.**

0 That exam wasn't bad. It was t*errible* !

1 I don't find History interesting. I find it f_____ !

2 That film wasn't funny. It was h_____ !

3 The water's not cold. It's f_____ !

4 No, the children weren't scared.
They were t_____ !

5 Their garden isn't big. It's e_____ !

6 Your writing isn't small. It's t_____ !

7 It isn't hot today. It's b_____ !

7 **Complete the second diary entry with extreme adjectives.**

January 1st, 2000

Life's pretty good. I can't really complain. I live in a big house with my parents. We get on well most of the time. I like school. It's interesting and I really enjoy going most days. Mrs Jackson, my Science teacher, is really funny. She makes me laugh and it's always fun in her lessons. In my spare time I go go-karting. It's a really exciting hobby. I won a trophy last week. It was pretty small, but the size isn't important. It says 'Most Improved Driver' on it, so I'm happy with it. I'm not sure my mum's so keen on my hobby. She's scared I'll have an accident. I tell her not to worry and that one day I'll be a world champion.

February 2nd, 2020

Life's pretty ¹_____ . I can't complain at all. I live in a ²_____ house with my wife and children. We get on well all of the time. I like my job. It's ³_____ and I really enjoy going most days. My boss is really ⁴_____ . He makes me laugh and it's always fun hanging out with him. I'm a racing driver. It's a really ⁵_____ sport. I won a trophy last week. It was ⁶_____ but the size isn't important. It says 'World Champion' on it so I'm ⁷_____ with it. I'm not sure my mum's so keen on my job. She's ⁸_____ I'll have an accident. I tell her, 'Isn't it time you stopped worrying?'

SUMMING UP

8 **Complete the dialogue with the words in the list. There are four you don't need.**

> amazing | career | degree
> enormous | huge | promote | retire
> settle | so | such | travel | terrible

Katie So what are your plans for the weekend, Joe?

Joe Well my dad's going to ¹_____ from work next week so we're having an ²_____ party for him on Saturday. I mean it's going to be really big!

Katie But he's ³_____ young!

Joe I know, and the crazy thing is that the company offered to ⁴_____ him too.

Katie So what made him decide to leave?

Joe Well the money he got was ⁵_____ but it was ⁶_____ a stressful job.

Katie Yes, money isn't everything.

Joe Now he's got plans to ⁷_____ the world with Mum.

Katie But what about you?

Joe Well, I hope they're going to wait until I'm at university doing a ⁸_____ . But the mood Dad's in, I can't be too sure!

C HOW PEOPLE BEHAVE
Personality

1 Complete the sentences with the missing adjectives.

1 He only thinks about himself and what's good for him. He's really s_____ .

2 She always says 'please' or 'thank you'. She's very p_____ .

3 You didn't need to buy me a present. That was very t_____ of you.

4 He's a very c_____ person. He never panics.

5 She's very l_____ . She always seems to have so much energy.

6 He's very g_____ with his time and is always happy to help us.

7 Libby's very quiet but she isn't unfriendly. I think she's just a bit s_____ .

8 Jack hasn't replied to my message yet which I think is a bit r_____ .

Using *should*

2 Write a reply to each sentence using *should* or *shouldn't*.

0 'I'm really tired today.'
You should have gone to bed earlier.

1 'It's Toni's birthday tomorrow.'
_____

2 'I can't believe it. We've missed the train.'
_____

3 'My tooth is really hurting.'
_____

4 'Mia's really upset with me.'
_____

5 'I'm bored.'
_____

3 Complete the dialogue. Use *should / shouldn't have* and the correct form of the verbs in the list.

| bring | get up | put | set | stay |

Teacher Have you done your homework, Lily?

Lily Umm, I have but I left it at home.

Teacher But it was for today. You ¹_____ it with you.

Lily I know. I'm sorry but I was in such a hurry I left it on the kitchen table.

Teacher You ²_____ earlier. Then you wouldn't have been in such a hurry.

Lily I know. I ³_____ my alarm clock but I forgot. And I ⁴_____ my book in my bag the night before. And I ⁵_____ up so late last night.

Career paths

4 Complete the crossword and find the mystery profession.

1 They take all the rubbish from the roads.

2 My sister builds bridges and tunnels.

3 She tries to help people who find themselves in trouble with the police.

4 She looks after a 4-year-old and two 6-year-olds.

5 My mum works in a really busy hospital in the middle of London.

6 He gets us to and from school.

5 Choose the correct options.

1 My uncle is a receptionist in a clinic. He works in *finance / healthcare*.

2 My whole family work in *public service / management*. Dad's a nurse, Mum's a teacher and my uncle is a policeman.

3 I'd like to work in *law / education*, maybe in a school or a university.

4 If you want to find a job, you'll need the right *qualifications / salary*.

5 There are more than 500 *employees / employers* working at the factory.

6 They're one of the biggest *employees / employers* in the region. More than 2,000 people work for them.

7 My mum's in *education / finance*. She's an accountant at the hospital.

8 I know he's in *law / healthcare*. He's a solicitor, I think.

Decisions

6 Match the parts of the sentences.

1 Come on, Alice. Make up ☐

2 Can you be quiet? I find it difficult to make ☐

3 It's an important decision. I need to think long ☐

4 Don't worry. You can always change ☐

5 It's been ten minutes already. Have you come ☐

a and hard about it.

b your mind later if you want to.

c your mind. Do you want a sandwich or not?

d to a decision yet?

e a decision when people are talking.

Permission

7 **Choose the correct options.**

1 Do your parents *allow* / *let* / *make* you take your phone to bed at night?
2 I'm not *allowed* / *let* / *made* to go out on a school night.
3 My parents *let* / *make* / *allow* me do my homework before I can play on the tablet.
4 Our teacher *makes* / *lets* / *allows* us do a vocabulary test every day.
5 My mum won't *allow* / *let* / *make* me come to your party.
6 Are we really *allowed* / *let* / *made* to go to the music festival this summer?

8 **Complete the missing words.**

1 Are you _____ to stay up late at the weekend?
2 Does your teacher _____ you use phones in class?
3 Do your parents _____ you do your homework before you can watch TV?
4 Are you _____ to do any housework by your parents?
5 Do your parents _____ you to get up late in the holidays?
6 Do your teachers _____ you eat in class?

9 **Write your answers to the questions in Exercise 8.**

SUMMING UP

10 **Put the sentences in order to make a dialogue.**

Tim I hope you're right. Anyway, I'm allowed to use their family car.

Tim Have you heard the news? I've got a summer job.

Tim I'm actually quite scared. I don't really have much experience with kids.

Tim I don't think I'm allowed to use it when I'm not working.

Tim Childminding for children from the same family every day.

Lucy Wow. You're very brave.

Lucy You'll be fine. You're kind and lively. That's all kids want.

Lucy You never know. You should ask them. A friend with a car! This is going to be a good summer.

Lucy Cool! Where are you going to take me?

Lucy Congratulations. What is it?

D NEW THINGS
Reporting verbs

1 **Match each verb with a sentence.**

> agree | demand | encourage | explain
> invite | persuade | recommend | refuse

1 To get to the station, you need to take the number 3 bus. _____
2 No, Bella, I won't take you to the party. _____
3 I want you to get out of my house, Ben. Now! _____
4 Would you like to go to the cinema, Jenny? _____
5 Come on, Lukas. Come to the party with me. You will? Great! _____
6 You should enter the talent show. You're brilliant at singing, Lucie. _____
7 Read this book, Matt. You'll love it. _____
8 OK, Simon. I'll talk to your dad and see if I can change his mind. _____

2 **Put the sentences in Exercise 1 into reported speech.**

1 He *explained how to get to the station by bus.*
2 She _____
3 He _____
4 She _____
5 He _____
6 She _____
7 He _____
8 She _____

3 **Complete the text with the reporting verbs in Exercise 1. There are three you don't need.**

I can't believe I've ¹_____ to do a parachute jump with Tim. How did that happen? It all started when he ²_____ to me about this children's charity that he is involved with. I said it sounded interesting and he ³_____ me along to one of their meetings. So I went to see what it's all about. I didn't know they were organising a sponsored parachute jump. They asked me to get involved and of course I ⁴_____ . I mean, I'm not mad. But they kept on trying to ⁵_____ me to do it and in the end, I gave in and said 'yes'. And now I can't get out of it.

Negative adjectives

4 Rewrite the sentences using a negative adjective.

0 I'm not happy.
   I'm unhappy.

1 It isn't true.
   _____

2 It isn't a formal party.
   _____

3 They aren't patient.
   _____

4 That wasn't responsible of you.
   _____

5 Buy it. It isn't expensive.
   _____

6 They aren't polite children.
   _____

7 I don't think that's possible.
   _____

Changes

5 Match the parts of the sentences.

1 If you're bored, why don't you take ☐
2 The children are all doing ☐
3 If children form ☐
4 If he doesn't change his ☐
5 Why's it so difficult to break ☐
6 I'm not going to make ☐
7 I'm finding physics too hard.
   I might give ☐
8 Sometimes I struggle ☐

a any resolutions this new year.
b up having lessons.
c to understand maths. It can be so hard.
d bad habits?
e good habits when they're young, they'll
   never forget them.
f up a new hobby?
g ways, he's going to get into trouble one day.
h really well at their new school.

Regrets: *I wish ... / If only ...*

6 For each situation write one present regret and one past regret.

0 I can't afford to buy my mum a birthday present.
   I wish I had more money.
   If only I hadn't spent all my money on clothes.

1 Sara refuses to speak to me.
   _____
   _____

2 I'm so tired. I want to go to bed, but I'm stuck here in my Science lesson.
   _____
   _____

3 All my friends are in the school football team.
   _____
   _____

4 I'm bored.
   _____
   _____

SUMMING UP

7 Complete the dialogue with the words/phrases in the list. There are four you don't need.

> encourage | struggle | wasn't | unhappy
> am not | impossible | take up | gave up
> demand | impolite | hadn't given it up | refuse

Martha What's up, Ben? You look a bit
   [1]_____ .

Ben I'm OK. I'm just bored. I've got nothing to do.

Martha Why don't you [2]_____ a new hobby? That will fill your time.

Ben Like what?

Martha Guitar lessons. You've always wanted to play the guitar better.

Ben That's true. I wish I [3]_____ when I was a teenager. I'd be really good now.

Martha Well, it's not too late to start again.

Ben It is. It's [4]_____ for someone my age to start learning an instrument.

Martha What! You're 23!

Ben I know, but I really [5]_____ with learning new things. I wish I [6]_____ that way, but I am.

Martha OK then – be bored.

Ben What! That's not very nice.

Martha Well, I'm trying to [7]_____ you, but you [8]_____ to listen. I give up.

Ben I'm sorry, Martha. I'm just joking. And, you're right – it's never too late to start something new. In fact, I think I might just do that. Do you know any good teachers?

Martha That's more like it. Actually, I do ... My brother! He's great.

1 SURVIVAL INSTINCT

GRAMMAR
Verbs followed by infinitive or gerund
→ SB p.14

1 ★☆☆ **Complete the table with the words in the list according to what they are followed by (infinitive or gerund).**

ask | can't stand | choose
decide | detest | don't mind
enjoy | keep | manage | miss
offer | promise | suggest | want

infinitive	gerund
ask	

2 ★★☆ **Circle the correct options.**

1 **Molly** Did Simon manage *to finish / finishing* his essay last night?

Harry Yes, so he's promised *coming / to come* climbing with us this weekend.

Molly Fantastic. My dad's offered *to give / giving* us a lift to the climbing club.

2 **Nora** I suggested *to take / taking* a picnic, but they don't want *to carry / carrying* it.

Sam I don't mind *to carry / carrying* it.

3 **Elif** Now I live in the city, I miss *to go / going* for long walks in the countryside.

Jo Really? I can't stand *to walk / walking* in the countryside.

4 **Anna** You're very good at the violin!

Zoe No, I'm not. I really enjoy *to play / playing* and I keep *to practise / practising*, but I'm not getting any better.

Anna Ask Tom *to help / helping* you. He's a brilliant musician.

5 **Josh** You'll never guess what? Max came climbing with us.

Ellie But Max detests *to climb / climbing*!

3 ★★☆ **Complete the text with the correct form of the verbs in brackets.**

I enjoy [1]_____ (climb) mountains, so last year I decided [2]_____ (climb) Ben Nevis in Scotland with a friend. We planned [3]_____ (go) to Scotland in August and we arranged [4]_____ (stay) with a friend in Fort William for a few days. We started our climb at 6 am and we hoped [5]_____ (get back) down the mountain by 2 pm. The weather was good, so we managed [6]_____ (reach) the summit in two hours. We never imagined [7]_____ (see) such a beautiful view from the summit. The next day, we felt like [8]_____ (climb) Ben Nevis again.

4 ★★★ **Find and correct five mistakes in the dialogue.**

Kate I can't believe it. I managed climbing Devil's Rock this weekend.

Matt Did you? That's great.

Kate I've watched you climb it a couple of times, but I never imagined to climb it myself. I'm hoping doing more climbing next weekend. I learned going down the rock face using a rope. That was scary! What did you do at the weekend?

Matt I wanted coming climbing with you and the others, but I had some homework to do.

5 ★★★ **Complete the sentences so that they are true for you.**

1 I enjoy _____

2 I started _____

3 I don't mind _____

4 I hate _____

5 I refuse _____

6 I love _____

Verbs which take gerund and infinitive with different meanings: *remember, try, stop, regret, forget* → SB p.15

6 ★☆☆ Match the sentences with their meanings.

1 I stopped to look at the view. ☐
2 I stopped looking at the view. ☐
3 He remembers buying a newspaper. ☐
4 Remember to buy a newspaper, Tom. ☐
5 He tried learning Chinese. ☐
6 He tried to learn Chinese. ☐
7 I'll never forget reading that comment on your post. ☐
8 I forgot to read that article online. ☐

a I'll always remember reading that comment on your post.
b He knows he bought a newspaper.
c I didn't remember to read that article online.
d He wasn't able to learn Chinese.
e I didn't look at the view any more.
f Don't forget to buy a newspaper.
g I stopped so I could look at the view.
h His goal was to impress his clients by speaking Chinese.

7 ★★☆ Complete the dialogues with the correct form of the verbs.

1 A I forgot _____ (tell) you. We're going to London this weekend.
   B Lucky you!
2 A Did Helena finish her essay?
   B No, she didn't. She tried _____ (finish) it last night, but she couldn't.
3 A I regret _____ (not leave) earlier on Saturday.
   B Yes, you missed the boat race.
4 A Do you still play the piano?
   B No, I stopped _____ (play) when I was nine.
5 A Do you remember _____ (lend) me that book?
   B Yes, I do. You haven't given it back yet.
6 A You left your guitar at Olivia's house. Her mum rang me this morning.
   B Yes, I know. I stopped _____ (pick it up) on the way home.

8 ★★☆ Complete the sentences with the correct form of the verbs.

eat | listen | tell | watch

1 I was revising for the History exam and then I stopped _____ to some music.
2 I listened to the first three songs and then I stopped _____ .
3 I remember _____ that film last year.
4 Remember _____ that film tonight. It's really good.
5 I've tried _____ more vegetables, but I don't like them.
6 I tried _____ pineapple covered in chocolate, but it tasted really weird.
7 I regret _____ you that there aren't any more tickets for the match.
8 I regret _____ Emma about the trip last weekend.

9 ★★★ Write a sentence that is true for you for each of the situations.

1 Something you regret doing or saying.
_____
2 Something you remember doing or saying when you were in primary school.
_____
3 Something you have tried doing.
_____
4 Something you have stopped doing.
_____
5 Something you forgot to do recently.
_____

GET IT RIGHT!

Infinitive or gerund after certain verbs

Learners often forget to use the infinitive or the gerund after certain verbs.

✓ Sam and Alfie decided to go out for a meal.
✗ Sam and Alfie decided go out for a meal.

Correct the mistake in each sentence.

1 We couldn't afford do the survival course.
_____
2 He started feel a bit awkward as no one was talking to him.
_____
3 Ethan suggested have an early night before the exam.
_____
4 I never promised help you with your homework!
_____
5 Do they practise to sing every evening?
_____
6 We wanted leave right away, but we couldn't.
_____

VOCABULARY
Verbs of movement

→ SB p.14

1 ★☆☆ **Find ten verbs of movement.**

O	C	L	I	M	B	T	T	T	H	P
D	S	S	A	Y	N	I	E	C	A	H
N	W	C	A	T	B	P	L	E	T	R
E	I	W	R	R	K	T	L	A	G	E
E	N	S	E	A	L	O	P	W	L	G
V	G	M	E	E	W	E	S	O	E	G
I	H	R	U	S	H	L	I	N	H	A
D	W	A	N	D	E	R	T	D	E	T
B	R	E	A	T	H	L	E	G	R	S

2 ★★☆ **Complete the text with the past tense of the verbs of movement in Exercise 1. There are two verbs you do not need to use.**

Jake ⁰_____*crawled*_____ through the tunnel on his hands and knees and then he ¹_____ over the wall. After that he held onto the rope and ²_____ across the river. He ³_____ very quietly past the house on the other side of the river. Then he quickly ⁴_____ up the mountain and slowly went down the other side in thick fog. After that, he ⁵_____ across the flat ground. He was in a hurry to finish now. Then suddenly, he fell and hurt his left leg, so he ⁶_____ on his right leg to the finish line. Everybody cheered. He ⁷_____ through the crowds of people and he shook hands with all his fans.

Adjectives to describe uncomfortable feelings

3 ★★☆ **Read the situations. How would you feel? Circle one of the adjectives.**

1 You don't know the answer to the next question on the exam paper. You can't do the next question until you've completed this one.
You are *stuck / puzzled*.

2 Last night you ate your brother's chocolate bar. He doesn't know yet.
You feel *guilty / desperate*.

3 You are at a party. Everybody knows each other, but you don't know anyone.
You feel *awkward / puzzled*.

4 You put your house keys on the desk. Now they aren't there.
You are *ashamed / puzzled*.

5 You shouted at one of your friends yesterday.
You feel *ashamed / guilty* of yourself.

6 You are locked in a room in a castle. You have no phone and there is no food. No one knows you are there.
You feel *desperate / stuck*.

4 ★★★ **Write a new situation for each feeling.**

1 puzzled
_____
_____

2 stuck
_____
_____

3 desperate
_____
_____

4 ashamed
_____
_____

5 guilty
_____
_____

6 awkward
_____
_____

WordWise:
Expressions with *right*

→ SB p.17

5 ★★☆ **Complete the dialogues with the phrases in the list.**

right | right away | right in the middle rightly or wrongly

1 A _____ , we now have to wear school uniform.
B I know. I don't agree with it.

2 A Where's the new cinema?
B It's _____ of town, next to the theatre.

3 A Can I come with you and Sam to the match on Saturday?
B Yes, of course.
A You're setting off early, _____ ?
B Yes, we're leaving at eight o'clock.

4 A Abby's just messaged about the concert on Saturday. Do we want tickets?
B Yes, we do.
A I'll message her back _____ , then.

REFERENCE

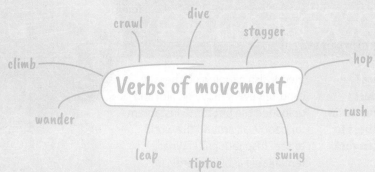

Verbs of movement

crawl | dive | stagger | hop | rush | climb | wander | leap | tiptoe | swing

ADJECTIVES TO DESCRIBE UNCOMFORTABLE FEELINGS

ashamed   guilty

awkward   puzzled

desperate   stuck

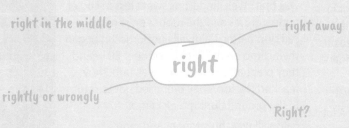

right

right in the middle | right away | rightly or wrongly | Right?

VOCABULARY EXTRA

1   **Match the verbs with the pictures.**

march | slide | soar | sprint | tumble

1 _____   2 _____   3 _____

4 _____   5 _____

2   **Complete the adverts and posts with the correct verb.**

1 Can you hit a ball, run quickly and _____ across the ground? We need you NOW! Come and join our after-school soft ball club.

2 How do eagles _____ so high and how do they stay in the air? Find out the answers to this and lots more in tonight's *Science Talk*.

3 Improve your running and learn to _____ more quickly. Come along and talk to our coaches tomorrow at 6 pm.

4 Do you ever lose your balance and _____ over when you're standing on one leg? Try these simple techniques to improve your balance.

5 Can you help? Can you teach a group of us to _____ together and in time for our scout parade next weekend?

A Story of
Teamwork and
Perseverance

How do you climb a smooth rock face? In 2015, two young American climbers showed us how. Tommy Caldwell and Kevin Jorgeson became the first free climbers to climb the Dawn Wall of the El Capitan rock formation in California.

Free climbers don't use ropes when they climb. They only use their hands and feet. However, they do have ropes to hold them if they fall.

El Capitan is 914 metres high. That's almost 100 metres higher than the world's tallest building, the Burj Khalifa tower in Dubai, which has 163 floors. The climb took Caldwell and Jorgeson 19 days. They ate, drank and slept in small tents hanging from the rock face. They even read books there! They brewed coffee on special hanging stoves. Every few days, a friend on the ground climbed up on a rope and brought them new supplies of food and water.

So how do you climb a smooth rock face? A lot of it relies on the strength of your fingertips. Occasionally, the climbers needed to take a day off to stop and rest so that their fingertips could heal. To make their cuts heal more quickly, they used superglue and tape.

Unlike expeditions of a hundred years ago, people around the world were able to watch every moment of this climb as it happened. In their break times, the climbers updated their social media accounts and spoke to journalists on the phone. A photographer and good friend, also hanging off the wall, captured every move on film and uploaded the photos to Instagram for people all around the world to see. 'Inspirational' – 'What a remarkable achievement! I'm awed.' – 'Awesome! Amazing! And a true friendship!' – 'What bravery and courage!' These are just some of the comments that people tweeted as they watched the amazing climb.

A lot of the climbing was at night and it was all done in the middle of winter. Why was that? Well, fingertips sweat less in cooler temperatures and the rubber on shoes can grip better. Caldwell and Jorgeson began their climb on the 27th December 2014 and they planned to live on the wall until they reached the top. They promised not to return to the ground during their climb.

Caldwell was the stronger and more experienced climber and he was always ahead of Jorgeson. For ten days, Jorgeson continued to fall behind during his daily climbs. He knew that he was delaying his friend. But this climb was about teamwork and friendship. 'More than anything, I want to get to the top together,' said Caldwell on day 13. He couldn't imagine finishing without his friend. Finally on day 19, the two climbers made it to the top.

READING

1 **Read the article quickly and answer the questions.**

  1 Which body parts need to be very strong to free climb?

  2 What is the importance of the numbers 914, 19 and 27?

2 **Read the article again. Mark the sentences T (true) or F (false).**

  1 Caldwell and Jorgeson were the first free climbers to climb the wall. ☐

  2 El Capitan is in a national park in New Mexico. ☐

  3 El Capitan is a few metres shorter than the world's tallest building. ☐

  4 People all around the world were able to see pictures of the climb on social media. ☐

  5 The climbers' shoes grip better in warmer temperatures. ☐

  6 They started to climb the Dawn Wall in January 2015. ☐

  7 The two climbers decided not to descend to the ground until they had successfully reached the top of the Dawn Wall. ☐

  8 Caldwell wanted to finish the climb before his friend, Jorgeson. ☐

3 CRITICAL THINKING **Read the statements. Do you agree with them? Why / Why not? Think of reasons.**

  1 Mental strength is as important as physical strength in climbing.

  2 Teamwork is more important than individual achievements.

  3 True friendship is about sticking together through good times and bad.

4 **Many people tweeted as they watched the amazing climb. What comment would you have made?**

PRONUNCIATION
Diphthongs: alternative spellings
Go to page 118.

DEVELOPING {Writing}

A review for an adventure holiday

1 **INPUT** Read Elena's review quickly. Match the numbers with facts from the review.

1 80 million _____

2 5 _____

3 300 _____

2 **ANALYSE** Read Elena's review again. Circle the correct options.

1 Elena's style of writing is *formal / informal*.

2 Elena uses *some questions / very long sentences* in her review.

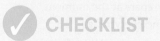

What's 80 million years old with lots of red sand? It's the Namib desert! It's the world's oldest desert. And guess what? I managed to walk across part of it this autumn. Not all of it though! It's 2,000 kilometres long.

The desert adventure was a fantastic experience. We travelled by jeep for some of it, but we walked at least five kilometres each day. That doesn't sound far, but walking on sand is really tough. I was exhausted when we finally reached the camp each evening. The walks were challenging for everyone. I was with my parents and my older brother. It was a three-day trek and we spent two icy cold nights camping. We wandered across the sand with our guide and saw 900-year-old trees. We climbed up a mountain of sand – it was more than 300 metres high – and the views were spectacular. I forgot to take my phone, so I didn't get any pictures of the amazing orange and red sunsets or the incredible wildlife. The experience was unforgettable and the whole trip was confidence-building. I think I could face any challenge now.

Any tips? Yes. Remember to take a hat and a water bottle. The heat of the sun is fierce during the day. And prepare yourself for a challenging few days!

3 **Read the review again. Answer the questions.**

1 How does Elena describe the Namib desert?

_____

2 How did Elena feel when she reached the camp each evening?

_____

3 Who did Elena go with?

_____

4 How did Elena feel after the trip?

_____

5 What tips does Elena give?

_____

4 **Find the adjectives (1–5) in the review. Write what the adjectives describe. Then think of another adjective you could use instead.**

Adjective	What it describes	My new choice of adjective
1 tough	*walking on sand*	
2 exhausted		
3 icy cold		
4 spectacular		
5 fierce		

5 **PLAN** **Think about a holiday you have been on (or invent a holiday). Make notes for each paragraph.**

- Introductory paragraph – Where was it? What did you do? When?
- Main body – What was the experience like? How did you feel? Who were you with? How did you feel after?
- Conclusion – What travel tips do you have?

6 **PRODUCE** **Write a review of your holiday (200–250 words). Use your notes in Exercise 5. Make sure you include all the points in the checklist.**

✓ **CHECKLIST**

Use informal language and some questions.
Include interesting adjectives.
Use verbs of movement.
Include an introductory paragraph, a main body, a conclusion and some travel tips.

LISTENING

1 🔊 1.02 **Read the sentences. Then listen and match the dialogues (1–3) with the sentences (a–c).**

a They are in the middle of a challenge. One of them wants to give up. ☐

b They have done a survival weekend and they want a new challenge. ☐

c They watch a video about people lying or kneeling on surfboards and using their arms to move. ☐

DIALOGUE

1 **Complete the dialogues with the phrases in the list.**

> I bet you | I bet you I | I challenge you
> I'll never manage to
> I think you're probably right | No problem
> Of course you can | that's too easy

1 **Oli** Wow! Did you see that? _____ can't do that.

Ben _____ can.

Oli All right. _____ to kneel on the kitchen table, but imagine you're on water.

Ben But _____ .

Oli Go on then. Show me.

2 **Oscar** You go on ahead, Beth. _____ climb up to the top of those trees and then get to the next platform.

Beth _____ , Oscar. Come on. Keep going. You're doing really well. I bet you can climb up there faster than I can.

3 **Jake** It was a physical and mental challenge, but I'm glad I've done it.

Luisa Same here. What's our next challenge? I bet we can do a longer survival course, like a whole week.

Jake _____ . It won't be until next summer, though. I don't think we're ready for it just yet and we don't have enough time to prepare at the moment, with our exams and everything.

Luisa _____ . We definitely need more practice before we do a course for a week. But at least we know we've both found our inner survivors!

2 🔊 1.02 **Listen again and complete each sentence with one word.**

1 Oli wants Ben to come and watch a _____ .

2 Paddle boarding started in the _____ .

3 Oscar can't continue because he can't climb to the top of the _____ .

4 The weather's very bad. It's just started to _____ .

5 Jake enjoys being _____ .

6 The weekend was a physical and _____ challenge for Jake.

PHRASES FOR FLUENCY ⟶ SB p.18

1 **Match the parts of the phrases.**

1 same ☐   a a shout
2 something ☐   b what?
3 give me ☐   c deal
4 you know ☐   d were we?
5 where ☐   e here
6 it's a ☐   f or other

2 **Complete the dialogues with phrases from Exercise 1.**

1 **A** Come along to the indoor climbing club and I'll teach you. I'm a trainer there.

B _____ . When do I start?

2 **A** Dinner's not ready yet.

B OK. _____ when it's ready.

3 **A** Rob's going on an adventure holiday this September. It's a trek across the desert in Jordan.

B I know. I thought he was crazy at first. But _____ ? Now I think I want to go with him. It's a real challenge.

4 **A** Sorry about that, Matt. I had to answer a call. Now, _____ ?

B You were just showing me the route for Saturday's trek.

A Ah, yes.

5 **A** I'm sorry I haven't called you this week. I've had a lot of things to do.

B _____ . I've been really busy with the band.

6 **A** Have you seen Kate recently?

B No. She's at football training or tennis club or _____ .

READING AND USE OF ENGLISH
Part 5: Multiple Choice

You are going to read an article about survival skills in the forest. For questions 1–6, choose the answer (A, B, C or D) which you think fits best according to the text.

A NIGHT IN THE FOREST

I didn't think I was afraid of the dark, but then it's not often that I find myself wandering around a forest at night – on my own. My eyes start to play tricks on me: shadows move between bushes, insects buzz, a solitary owl hoots, and I'm a little bit lost. What would Ged Lawless do? Ged is the former soldier who runs the UK Survival School. He's been teaching me how to find my way at night. This is my first attempt at going it alone. He's out there in the forest somewhere, and I know that if I start shouting, or call his mobile number, he'll come and rescue me, but really, that's not why I'm here.

As Ged explained earlier in the day, if you really get lost at night, the most sensible thing to do would be to stay put until dawn. Apparently, the area underneath a holly bush provides a good, if spiky, temporary shelter – they're dense, and evergreen. Quite apart from avoiding the risk of tripping over things, you'd have a better idea of direction – although you'd be amazed how many people don't know that the sun rises in the East – or what that means in terms of finding your way. Anyway, I'm slowly getting used to the forest's spookiness, and I'm not going to admit defeat yet. I'm pretty sure I can find my own way out.

There's always a point in films when a person who's lost in the desert or in the snow, dehydrated and exhausted, comes across a set of their own footprints and realises they've just walked in a huge exhausting circle. Apparently, this happens in real life too. A research study in Germany found that unless people have the sun, the moon or landmarks to give them a point of reference,

this tends to be the case. The researchers originally thought this was because everybody has one leg that is slightly longer or stronger than the other. But scientists now think that's wrong; that lots of small errors of judgement in the brain stop people from identifying 'straight ahead' correctly without something to help them.

If you already know which direction you need to go in, there are several ways to find this in the dark, and by far the best is to establish north using the stars. For this you do need to know a bit of basic astronomy, but I reckon I could manage **it.** Tonight is very cloudy, however, so I'm not in luck. It is quite windy though. I remember Ged saying: 'Keep in mind that almost all of our weather here in the British Isles comes from a south-westerly direction. Unless it's a bitterly cold wind, in which case it could be coming from the opposite direction. But tonight we just have a warm breeze, so that tells me which way is south-west. To double-check, I throw some strands of dried grass up into the air and see which way they blow.

Having set my mind to it, I'm sure I could have made it back to Ged with no real problem, but unfortunately it wasn't to be. After about half an hour he starts calling my name with a note of slight panic in his voice, and I can see his head torch glinting between the trees in the distance. Remembering his advice for picking such a point and heading straight towards it, that is what I do.

1 From the first paragraph, we understand that the writer
   A is regretting having decided to come on a course.
   B hasn't followed all her course leader's instructions.
   C is taking part in an outdoor activity as part of a course.
   D has become separated from the other participants on a course.

2 Why does the writer decide to keep moving in the dark forest?
   A She lacks the confidence to build herself a shelter.
   B She's unsure that daylight would help her very much.
   C She's keen to prove that somebody is wrong about her.
   D She doesn't want to give up the challenge she's been set.

3 What do we learn from the article about some research in Germany?
   A It reached a conclusion that has since been questioned.
   B It established why some people are more likely to get lost.
   C It showed that a situation commonly seen in films is unrealistic.
   D It failed to take into account physical differences between people.

4 What does the word 'it' in bold refer to in paragraph 4?
   A a knowledge of astronomy
   B using the stars to find north
   C dealing with weather conditions
   D using several natural clues in the dark

5 The writer uses dried grass in order to confirm that
   A the direction of the wind doesn't keep changing.
   B there is enough wind for her to reach a conclusion.
   C her assumptions about the wind direction are correct.
   D the wind is moving in the same direction as the clouds.

6 From the end of the article, we understand that the writer is
   A disappointed not to have achieved her goal.
   B amused that the course leader can't find her.
   C relieved that the experience is coming to an end.
   D determined to find the way without anyone's help.

2 ON THE ROAD

Grammar video

▶ 05

(G) GRAMMAR
Relative clauses (review) ⟶ SB p.22

1 ★★☆ **Complete the gaps with *who, which* or *that*. Mark the relative clauses D (defining) or ND (non-defining).**

0 People _____ who _____ move to a big city can find it hard to meet people. `D`

1 My sister Libby, _____ lives in New York, has made a lot of friends there. ☐

2 The café, _____ opened near the university, is a good place to meet people. ☐

3 Isaac, _____ has just moved in next door to me, has four sisters. ☐

4 It's not always easy to meet people _____ like the same things as you. ☐

5 Of the six flats, the one _____ Sally shares with four friends is the smallest. ☐

2 ★★☆ **Find and correct the mistake in each sentence.**

0 I'm very proud of my mother who works for a local charity.
I'm very proud of my mother, who works for a local charity.

1 This is a photograph who I took in Italy.
_____

2 The boy which bought my bike lives in this street.
_____

3 My mother who is a doctor often has to work at weekends.
_____

4 I've got a new phone who is far better than my old one.
_____

5 The music artist, who had the most streamed track in 2019, was Lewis Capaldi.
_____

6 I don't really like people, who talk a lot.
_____

which to refer to a whole clause ⟶ SB p.22

3 ★☆☆ **Write sentences from the prompts, using *which*.**

0 Some people / listen / to very loud music / can / damage / their ears
Some people listen to very loud music, which can damage their ears.

1 We / walk / to school / is / good / for our health
_____
_____

2 My grandparents / go to Spain / three times a year / means / they / practise their Spanish
_____
_____

3 Some blind people / have / guide dogs / gives / them more independence
_____
_____

4 My sister / spends / hours / working / on the computer / sometimes / gives / her / a headache
_____
_____

4 ★★☆ **Match the ideas. Then write sentences using *which*.**

0 bus to school / cost £2.50 `b`
1 I like / watch films at home ☐
2 friend / going / live in Colombia ☐
3 brother's phone / stolen last week ☐
4 famous band / play in our town next week ☐

a be / big change in lifestyle
b be / very expensive for me
c not happen / very often
d mean / not able to / message people
e be / cheaper / go / cinema

0 *The bus to school costs £2.50, which is very expensive for me.*

1 _____
2 _____
3 _____
4 _____

Omitting relative pronouns → SB p.25

5 ★☆☆ **Complete the gaps with *that, which, who* or – if the pronoun is not necessary.**

1 Nico paid back the money _____ he owed me last week.

2 I know a lot of people _____ have eaten at that restaurant.

3 There are a few things _____ I want to keep with me.

4 This is the book _____ Lily gave me for my birthday.

5 These aren't the photos _____ were in the newspaper.

6 I'm the sort of person _____ likes to spend time alone.

6 ★★☆ **Complete the dialogue with *who, which, that* or – if the pronoun is not necessary.**

Sophia George, you've moved a lot. What are the things ¹_____ you think are important about moving?

George Yes, well, I think the thing ²_____ is most important is to be optimistic about the move. Of course, there are things ³_____ you'll miss, but think of all the exciting things there will be. New places, new people!

Sophia But what about my friends? This is the only place ⁴_____ I've ever lived in!

George You can keep in touch with the people ⁵_____ are your most important friends. And you can visit – you're going to live in Ireland, right? Not on the moon!

Sophia I know, but you need to take a train and then the ferry, ⁶_____ makes it complicated and expensive. And what if I don't make new friends?

George Look, don't worry! You're an outgoing person ⁷_____ makes friends quickly – you'll be OK. But you know, one thing ⁸_____ I like to do before I move is make a scrapbook ⁹_____ will remind me of the place and the people. I put photos, names, birthdays and email addresses in it, ¹⁰_____ helps me to keep in touch with the friends ¹¹_____ I've made.

Sophia That's a great idea! Thanks, George.

Reduced relative clauses → SB p.25

7 ★★☆ **Join the sentences to make one sentence using reduced relative clauses.**

0 Catarina is an Italian student. She is studying English in London.
Catarina is an Italian student studying English in London.

1 Andi fell and hurt himself. He was painting a wall.
_____
_____

2 We travelled with two students. They were going to Paris.
_____
_____

3 I met a French student on the train. He was travelling to London.
_____
_____

4 A scientist accidentally discovered Post-It notes. He was trying to invent a strong glue.
_____
_____

5 My sister found a wallet. It was lying in the street.
_____
_____

GET IT RIGHT!

which and who

A common error for learners is to use *which* instead of *who* (or vice versa) in relative clauses.

✓ I met some friendly people **who** became friends of mine.

✗ I met some friendly people *which* became friends of mine.

Complete the sentences with *which* or *who*.

1 Please let me know _____ is the most direct way to the conference.

2 Most of the students _____ worked hard did well in their exams.

3 The motorists _____ use this road are kindly asked to drive more slowly.

4 There are a lot of people moving to this area, _____ means there will be fewer parking places.

5 Sam had a year out in Italy, _____ is a beautiful country.

6 Lucy turned out to be someone _____ you can rely on.

7 The Aboriginal Australians, _____ have been living there for more than 40,000 years, have their own languages.

8 The food _____ we cooked was a mixture of different recipes, but it tasted great!

VOCABULARY
Groups of people

→ SB p.22

1 ★★☆ **Complete the crossword.**

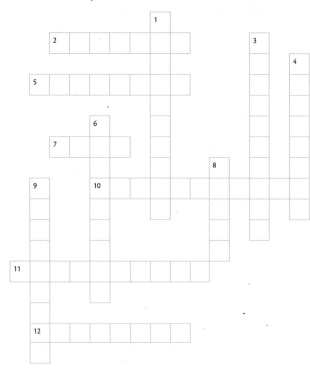

Across

2 Albert Einstein fled to the US from Germany and was a ... .

5 My mum works from home so she isn't a ... .

7 The plane was carrying 90 passengers and seven ... members.

10 It's a huge city – there are about 12 million ... here.

11 She's an important ... and hopes to become the leader of her party soon.

12 The factory is the town's biggest ... .

Down

1 You can't drive here – this is a ... zone.

3 The US is often called a nation of ... because so many families originally came from other countries.

4 The accident was caused by a ... who was driving too fast.

6 Big, noisy lorries use this street, and some ... are unhappy about it.

8 There are more than 30 teachers on the ... of the school.

9 It's a really big company – there are more than 1,000 ... there.

2 ★★☆ **Which people might say these things?**

1 'Cyclists – they're terrible, I can't stand them.'

_____

2 'The boss is OK but she makes us work really hard too!'

_____

3 'I promise that we will make this country better.'

_____

4 'It isn't always easy to make a new start in another country.'

_____

5 'We really love living here – it's great.'

_____

Phrasal verbs (1)

→ SB p.24

3 ★☆☆ **Choose the correct options.**

1 I thought the exam would be difficult, but it *turned out / brought about* to be easy.

2 Let's *pick up / set out for* the concert now. It's going to be busy.

3 The neighbours are so noisy – I can't *go through / put up with* it any more.

4 We complained so much that we *brought about / picked up* some changes.

5 I don't really speak Japanese – I just *picked up / put up with* some phrases.

6 We're due to *touch down / wear out* any minute now.

7 I worked really hard on Monday – I was *turned out / worn out*.

8 Don't worry – it's just a bad time I'm *wearing out / going through*.

4 ★★☆ **Complete each sentence with one or two words.**

1 What time do we need to set _____ the station in the morning?

2 They walk so quickly that they wear me _____ !

3 Everyone said it was going to rain, but it turned _____ to be a lovely day.

4 I'm going to hang _____ my friends this afternoon.

5 Be nice to her – she's going _____ a bad time right now.

6 He's never had French lessons – he just picked it _____ in France.

7 We hope these changes will bring _____ some better results.

8 When will the next rocket _____ on the moon?

PRONUNCIATION
Phrasal verb stress Go to page 118.

REFERENCE

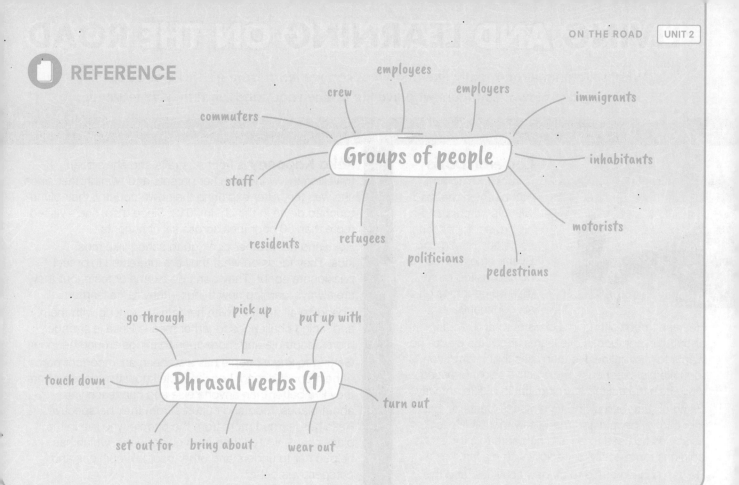

Groups of people

employees
crew
employers
immigrants
commuters
inhabitants
staff
motorists
residents
refugees
politicians
pedestrians

Phrasal verbs (1)

go through
pick up
put up with
touch down
turn out
set out for
bring about
wear out

 VOCABULARY EXTRA

1 Match the words with the pictures.

board | cast | household | squad | troupe

1 _____ 2 _____

3 _____ 4 _____ 5 _____

2 Complete the sentences with words from Exercise 1.

1 The _____. of directors has to approve all the decisions.
2 Three of our _____ have injuries and can't play in the match today.
3 Everyone loved the dance _____ that won the competition.
4 My best friend's pet cat is an important part of their _____ .
5 After our final school performance, there was a big party for the whole _____ .

3 Read the sentences. Which group of people are they talking about?

1 We have 11 players for the match, so don't worry if you can't make it.
_____

2 The acrobats were my favourite at last night's circus performance.
_____

3 We all do chores. I usually lay the table. _____

4 They were all amazing, especially since some of them have never acted before. _____

5 The director has to make the final decision about our proposal. Let's see what she says.
_____

21

LIVING AND LEARNING ON THE ROAD

What's life on the road really like and what can we learn from it? This week's special feature looks at two teenagers who live life on the road, and what they've learned.

Cameron Davis

is from Toronto and he's been on the road with his parents and his brother for as long as he can remember. By the time he was 13, he had visited more than 45 countries on six continents.

He hasn't been sitting in a classroom and reading about things in books. He learns about the places he wants to visit online. He then uses that information to make his experience more active and interesting while he's there. He's learning, but in a different way.

Being on the road all the time means Cameron has met a lot of people and made new friends. He isn't as shy as he used to be and he's able to express his opinions more easily, especially with his family.

He hasn't been afraid to try new activities, and this has helped build his confidence. He also enjoys trying different kinds of food.

Seeing households where people depend on each other to survive means that Cameron looks at things from a different perspective now. He understands more about sharing chores like cooking and cleaning.

Cameron also takes more responsibility now. For example, he packs his own suitcase. If he forgets something, he can't blame his parents! He knows travel involves risks, but it's about choosing the good risks and becoming more independent.

Réka Kaponay

is from Australia and she's been travelling the world with her parents and twin brother since she was ten. After exploring their own country, their plane touched down in the US in 2012. Since then, she's visited more than 50 countries across six continents.

Réka and her brother don't go to school like most kids. They focus on what they are interested in or feel passionate about. They don't do exams or tests, but they are always learning new things – they're life learners.

Spending all her time with her family, working with them and facing challenges together means Réka is stronger, more adaptable and more open to things around her now.

Getting to know people has also been an important part of being on the road. Local people know the places where they live better than anyone else and can teach you about places, food and cultures from their perspective. Réka has learned more from the people who live in the places she's visited than from guidebooks, which has helped her to understand other people's opinions and perspectives better.

Réka has followed her dreams and she has written two books and has given talks on them. She wants to encourage other people to share stories, learn about each other's cultures and inspire other writers to tell their stories.

📖 READING

1 Read the article and tick (✓) the topics mentioned.

1 friends from home ☐
2 school and education ☐
3 keeping in touch with people ☐
4 learning from other people ☐
5 skills you develop ☐
6 speaking a different language ☐
7 telling stories ☐

2 Read the article again. Mark the questions C (Cameron), R (Réka) or B (both).

Who ...

1 has learned a lot outside a classroom? ☐
2 has become more independent? ☐
3 has become stronger as a result of different challenges? ☐
4 thinks taking risks is part of travel? ☐
5 wants to inspire other people, especially writers? ☐
6 has learned from other people to see things from a different perspective? ☐

3 CRITICAL THINKING Read the opinions. Do you agree with them? Why / Why not? Think of reasons.

1 'Education is better in schools and classrooms. You can't learn on the road.'
2 'Learning in the school of life won't help when you want to find a job in the future.'
3 'Teenagers need structure which they can only find through school.'
4 'Parents who travel round the world with their children are selfish. They're only thinking of themselves.'

4 Imagine you live life on the road. Write a short paragraph (50–80 words) about the most important thing you have learned so far.

DEVELOPING *Writing*

Writing an email to a friend

1 **INPUT** **Read Luka's email to Martha. Answer the questions.**

1 Where is he?

2 What is he doing there?

> **Luka**
> Luka@thinkmail.com
>
> Hi Martha,
> How's everything with you in England? ¹<u>Sorry I haven't written before</u>, but there's just been so much to do since I left Brazil to come here.
> And now here I am in Toronto, on my exchange year! You know that I'm staying with a family here, right? They're the Palliers, who live in an area called Glen Park. It's a few kilometres from the city centre, but there are buses and a subway, so ²<u>easy to get there</u>. The Palliers are very friendly and they've helped me settle in. They haven't got any kids, but I've made some friends my age round here and I do a language course in a language school three mornings a week and I've got friends there, too.
> Talking of language – well, that's been the tricky thing, especially listening. People don't talk like in the books at school! I mean, ³<u>no problem</u> when I'm talking to one person, but in a big group, it can be hard to follow the conversation. Still, it's getting easier!
> Otherwise, ⁴<u>all good</u>. I thought a lot of things would be very different here, but they aren't. One thing though, is the food. There are lots of Canadian restaurants. I didn't know anything about Canadian food before coming here. My favourite food so far are Nanaimo bars – they're like slices of cheesecake with chocolate on top. And you can have maple syrup with everything, but I think it's best on pancakes! Sport is different, too, and ice hockey is really popular. ⁵<u>Not like in Brazil</u>, where the national sport is definitely football!
> OK, ⁶<u>got to go</u>. Write and tell me how you are.
> Luka

2 **Read the email again and answer the questions.**

1 Why has he not written to Martha before now?

2 How does he travel from the Palliers' house into town?

3 How many children do the Palliers have?

4 How often does he do the language course?

5 Which types of Canadian food does he mention?

6 Which sport is popular in Canada?

3 **ANALYSE** **In some parts of the email, Luka left words out. Match the phrases (a–f) with the underlined parts (1–6).**

a there's ☐   d It's ☐

b I'm ☐   e I've ☐

c it's ☐   f it's ☐

✎ WRITING TIP

We often leave certain words out in informal speaking and writing (it's called **ellipsis**). It is usually the subject and the auxiliary verb that are left out, for example:

Did you have a nice weekend? becomes *Have a nice weekend?* (leaving out the subject *you* and the auxiliary *did*).

4 **What could be left out from these sentences? Rewrite the sentences.**

0 It's good to see you.
Good to see you.

1 There are no worries – we can do this easily.

_____

2 Are you having a good time?

_____

3 Do you see what I mean?

_____

5 **PLAN** **Imagine that you are doing an exchange programme in an English-speaking country. Make notes.**

Paragraph 1: Which country are you in?

Paragraph 2: Who are you staying with?

Paragraph 3: What difficulties have you had with the language?

Paragraph 4: Are there any cultural differences you've had to adjust to? What are they?

6 **PRODUCE** **Write an email to a friend about your experiences (200–250 words). Use your notes in Exercise 5. Make sure you include all the points in the checklist.**

✓ CHECKLIST

☐ Use an informal style.

☐ Include at least two examples of ellipsis.

☐ Mention language and cultural differences.

☐ Sign off and remind your friend to write back to you.

1 🔊 2.02 **Listen to two dialogues. Complete each sentence with between one and three words.**

1 1 Evie has won a _____ on social media.
   2 The prize is a _____-day trip to South Africa.
   3 She won't have to _____ on the trip.
   4 Max wants to know how many people _____ is for.
2 5 Monika and Lewis are looking at _____ comic books.
   6 Monika's grandfather collects _____ .
   7 He started his collection when he was _____ as a young man.
   8 _____ the money in his collection is old.

2 🔊 2.02 **Listen again. Complete these extracts with one or two words.**

1 **Evie** Well, in ¹_____ , I entered it. I kind of thought I knew lots of the answers, most of them in fact. And so I thought 'OK, why not?'
   Max And …? Hold on, you're not telling me …
   Evie Yes. I won! I heard today. I got a message and it said I'd won.
   Max That's ²_____ ! Wow. Well done. So, you've got a free trip to South Africa?
   Evie That's right. I can ³_____ it myself.
2 **Lewis** Do you collect anything, Monika?
   Monika No – but my grandfather's got ⁴_____ collection of money from all over the world. I think he's got coins and notes from ⁵_____ a hundred different countries.
   Lewis That's ⁶_____ collection!

DIALOGUE

1 **Put the sentences in order to make dialogues.**

1 ☐ A Go on – surprise me.
   ☐ A I hear you're going to Scotland for the weekend.
   ☐ A That's incredible.
   ☐ B Well, I got a return ticket for £57.50.
   ☐ B I know. It's amazing, isn't it? I could hardly believe it myself.
   ☐ B Yes, by train. I bought a really cheap ticket online last night. You'll never believe what I paid.

2 ☐ A Pretty interesting, I thought. You know, they move around with camels, and they can travel up to sixty kilometres a day.
   ☐ A Did you see the documentary last night about the Tuareg?
   ☐ A I know. And in that kind of heat. It's almost unbelievable.
   ☐ B No, I missed it. Was it any good?
   ☐ B I'm not sure I'd want to do it, I have to say.
   ☐ B Wow. That's quite a distance.

3 ☐ A In Alaska. And it's winter there. He wrote me an email – he said that sometimes, it's -25 degrees.
   ☐ A My friend Seb's gone travelling around the world.
   ☐ A I know. How do people survive in temperatures like that?
   ☐ B Really? I knew it got cold there, but not that cold!
   ☐ B I've got a better question. Why on earth did Seb choose to go somewhere so cold!?
   ☐ B Oh, right. So where is he now?

2 **Write two dialogues, each with six lines. Choose from these situations. In each of the dialogues, two friends are talking. Look at Exercise 1 to help you.**

1 One of them watched a football match. A player scored five goals.
2 One of them did an online quiz and got 49/50.
3 One of them has a new friend who is 2.12 metres tall.
4 One of them is saving to buy a musical instrument. It's very expensive.

Writing Part 2

1 Read the exam questions (1–3) and the tips (A–C). Complete the tips with the correct words: *article*, *email* or *review*.

2 Choose an exam task and write your article, email or review.

1 **Read the exam task. You see this announcement on an English-language website.**

THE BEST PLACE I'VE EVER VISITED

What's the best place you've ever visited?
When did you go? Who with? What did you like so much about it?
Write and tell us. Write about 140–190 words.
We'll publish the best articles on our website!
And there are prizes for the winners!

Write your article.

2 **Read the exam task.**

You spent some time studying English in a school in Britain or the US. You have received this email from the school director. Write your answer in 140–190 words in an appropriate style.

Dear …
I am writing to tell you that your exam results have arrived – you got an A. Congratulations, it's a great result!
I was wondering if you would like to return to us here at the school, and study for the examination at the next level up. We feel sure you would do very well in it.
Please write and let me know.
Best wishes
Julia Stevenson

Write your email.

3 **Read the exam task. You have seen an announcement in the school magazine.**

Book reviews wanted
Write a review of a book you have recently read. Your review should include the title and author's name, a brief description of the characters and the plot and themes of the book. Would you recommend this book to others? Give your opinion of the book. The best reviews will be published in the next edition of the magazine.

Write your review.

In part 2 you have to answer one of three questions. You have to write a text (140–190 words) from a choice of text types: an article for a magazine or a website, an email/letter, an essay or a review.

A Exam guide: writing a neutral / less informal _____

- Think about who you are writing to and the kind of language you should use.
- Plan what you want to say and how you will organise the content.
- Make sure you start and end with appropriate expressions.
- Make sure you include anything the task tells you to include.

B Exam guide: writing a _____

- Remember to include some adjectives to make your review interesting.
- Include some relevant vocabulary for a review, for example: *characters*, *plot*, *setting*, *themes*, etc.
- Your description of the plot needs to be clear and concise and you must be careful not to give the ending away.
- You need to choose a book that you have strong opinions about. Your opinion can be negative or positive.
- Explain who you would recommend the book to.

C Exam guide: writing an _____

Remember that you are writing for a magazine or website – it's for entertainment, rather than for information. So, try to make your writing lively and interesting. You can use:

- direct (rhetorical) questions.
- lots of adjectives and adverbs.
- sentences that are not too long and complicated.

CONSOLIDATION

🎧 LISTENING

1   🔊 2.03   **Listen to Amelia talking about her year in Indonesia. Put the things below in the order she mentions them. There are two she doesn't mention.**

☐ the food   ☐ the language
☐ her school   ☐ transport
☐ the weather   ☐ the people

2   🔊 2.03   **Listen again and mark the sentences T (true) or F (false).**

1   Amelia's dad was only going to spend half a year there.   ☐
2   The weather was always hot and dry.   ☐
3   Amelia's lost contact with most of her Indonesian friends.   ☐
4   She used to buy nasi goreng from a shop.   ☐
5   Amelia describes a *bejak* journey as being a bit dangerous, but exciting, too.   ☐

Ⓖ GRAMMAR

3   **Circle the correct options.**

1   I don't mind *to help / helping* you with your homework.
2   But, Dad, you promised *to take / taking* me to the cinema tonight!
3   I feel like *to eat / eating* some chocolate. I don't suppose you've got any?
4   Can I suggest *to take / taking* a break and finishing this later?
5   I really regret *to tell / telling* Paul all those things.
6   I bumped into Joshua on the high street and we stopped *to have / having* a chat.
7   I forgot *to post / posting* this letter again.
8   I don't remember *to invite / inviting* Ian to my party. Why's he here?

4   **Join the sentences to make one sentence.**

1   My sister spends all day on her phone. I find this very annoying.

_____

2   My favourite town is Brighton. It's on the south coast.

_____

3   I watched the film last night. I thought it was really boring.

_____

4   My best friend is Al. He was born on the same day as me.

_____

🅰🅩 VOCABULARY

5   **Match the parts of the sentences.**

1   I don't know how you put up   ☐
2   I'm ashamed of what I said and   ☐
3   Housework really wears me   ☐
4   I'm a bit stuck and   ☐
5   I wasn't in Spain long and I only picked   ☐
6   I felt a bit awkward and   ☐
7   It was a terrible thing to go   ☐
8   I can tell that he's guilty   ☐

a   out and makes me feel tired.
b   through and she doesn't like talking about it.
c   didn't know what to say.
d   by the look on his face.
e   could use some help.
f   with all his terrible jokes.
g   I want to say sorry.
h   up a few words of the language.

6   **Complete each word.**

1   We had to c_____ on our hands and knees.
2   The r_____ are really unhappy about the plans to open a new nightclub in the area.
3   The c_____ made sure all the passengers were safely off the ship before they left.
4   They w_____ around the city for hours. They had no idea where they were going.
5   She t_____ quietly up the stairs.
6   The c_____ were all very patient when the train was cancelled.
7   The company has more than 1,000 e_____ .
8   He grabbed the rope and s_____ across the river.

DIALOGUE

7 **Complete the dialogue with the phrases in the list.**

> I bet you can't | It's a deal | Of course I can | You know what?

Dan ¹_____ I don't think you could survive without your phone. We've only been in the restaurant 20 minutes and you've already checked it twice. In fact, ²_____ spend the rest of the meal without your phone.

George Don't be silly. ³_____ .

Dan OK, if you don't look at your phone until we finish eating, I'll pay for dinner.

George ⁴_____ . I hope you've got a lot of money with you.

READING

8 **Read the article and answer the questions.**

You would expect extreme sportspeople to be equipped with survival techniques. A mountaineer needs to be ready for a rapid descent in bad weather and a deep-sea diver needs to know what to do should they ever come face to face with a great white shark, for example. Even more everyday sportspeople need to know a few basic procedures and more than one football player's life has been saved by the actions of a quick-thinking team mate. But if there's one sport you would expect to be pretty safe, then it's golf. Golf courses are hardly the most dangerous of places. What could possibly go wrong there? Swedish golfer Daniela Holmqvist might have a thing or two to say about this. She was in Australia playing in a tournament when she felt a nasty bite on her lower leg. When she looked, she saw a small black spider on her ankle. She immediately brushed it away, but the pain was getting stronger and stronger. She quickly called for help and was told that she had been bitten by a black widow spider, one of the most poisonous creatures in the world. In fact, one bite can kill an adult in under an hour. The local people were very concerned and immediately called for medical help. But Daniela knew she could not afford to wait for it. She knew she had to do something there and then, as her leg had already started to swell. From out of her pocket she pulled a tee, the plastic object that a golfer uses to place the ball on at the start of each hole. Using the sharp end of the tee, she made a hole in her leg and squeezed the poison out from inside. It came flowing out in a clear liquid. Despite the pain, she kept applying pressure until all the fluid had been removed. Doctors were soon on the scene and helped bandage Daniela up. You might have thought that after a brush with death like this, you would want to go home and rest for a while. Not Daniela. Instead of taking any time off to recover, she insisted on finishing the remaining 14 holes to complete her game.

1 What dangers might a mountaineer or a deep-sea diver encounter?
_____

2 What dangers might a golfer encounter? _____

3 What danger did Daniela Holmqvist encounter?
_____

4 How did she react at first? _____

5 What did she do to survive the danger? _____

6 What did she do once the danger was over? _____

WRITING

9 **Think of a dangerous situation. Write a paragraph about how you would respond (160–180 words).**

Include:

- what the situation was
- what you did
- how you felt afterwards.

3 GROWING UP

◎ GRAMMAR
Quantifiers
⟶ SB p.32

1 ★☆☆ **Put the sentences in order (1–4) according to amount, 1 being the most.**

1 ☐ a She's got loads of cousins.
☐ b She's got a few cousins.
☐ c She's got several cousins.
☐ d She's got hardly any cousins.

2 ☐ a A small number of the children at our school go on to university.
☐ b None of the children at our school go on to university.
☐ c All of the children at our school go on to university.
☐ d The vast majority of children at our school go on to university.

3 ☐ a Mum hardly spends any time at home.
☐ b Mum spends plenty of time at home.
☐ c Mum doesn't spend much time at home.
☐ d Mum spends all her time at home.

2 ★★☆ **Complete the text with the words in the list.**

> all of | almost | deal | few
> hardly | loads | majority
> most | number | plenty | several

I love the street where we live. There are
⁰ _____loads_____ of houses and the vast
¹ _____ have families living
in them. That means there are always
² _____ of children to play with.
There are ³ _____ kids from my class
at school and ⁴ _____ us love football,
so ⁵ _____ days you'll find us playing
football in the park at the end of the street.
The park is great and I spend ⁶ _____
all of my time there. Of course, there are a small
⁷ _____ of my friends who don't like
playing football, but they usually come and join
us after the game. At the other end of the road
there are a ⁸ _____ shops where I
spend a good ⁹ _____ of my pocket
money on sweets. By Friday evening I've got
¹⁰ _____ any pocket money left!

3 ★★☆ **Choose the correct options.**

1 I'm crazy about dancing. I've posted *loads of / hardly any / a few* videos online.

2 There's no need to hurry. We've got *several / plenty / the vast majority* of time.

3 *Hardly any / Several / Good deal* of my friends study Geography. They prefer History.

4 There are *most / loads / all* of students going on the march.

5 The *vast majority / good deal / most* of students at our school speak two languages.

6 *All / A few / Majority* of my friends are watching that new series.

4 ★★★ **Complete the sentences using quantifiers so that they are true for you.**

1 I spend _____ my time _____ .

2 _____ my friends' _____ .

3 _____ the teachers at my school _____ .

4 _____ the children at my school _____ .

5 I spend _____ my money _____ .

6 I find _____ the subjects at school _____ .

so and *such* (review)
⟶ SB p.35

5 ★★☆ **Rewrite the sentences using the words in brackets.**

0 This is such a difficult question. (so)
This question is so difficult.

1 It's such a hot day today. (so) _____

2 My uncle's so generous. (such / man)
_____

3 Eliza's got so many gadgets. (such / a lot of)
_____

4 I ate so much. (such) _____

6 ★★★ **Write continuations for the sentences in Exercise 5.**

0 *This question is so difficult that I've no idea what the answer is.*

too and (not) enough
→ SB p.35

7 ★★☆ **Complete the sentence for each picture. Use *too* or *(not) enough*. Sometimes there is more than one possible answer.**

0   *We're only 16. We aren't old enough / we're too young.*

1   There are

_____

Will we get in?

2   Help! I can't do it,

_____

3   Maybe I've got

_____

or maybe I haven't got

_____!

do and did for emphasis
→ SB p.35

8 ★☆☆ **Match the sentences.**

1   Lucy did go to your party.   ☐
2   I did enjoy that meal.   ☐
3   Paolo did seem a little strange.   ☐
4   I do wish you'd turn down your music.   ☐
5   Amy looks really lovely in her new dress.   ☐
6   I do feel bad that you've lost your phone.   ☐

a   Is there anything wrong with him?
b   I'm trying to study.
c   Green does suit her.
d   She was wearing a red dress, remember?
e   But you can't borrow mine, sorry.
f   But I think I ate too much.

9 ★★☆ **Rewrite the sentences adding *do / does* or *did* to make them more emphatic.**

0   So you like my present!
    So you do like my present!

1   You know Tom. You met him at Charlie's party, remember?

_____

2   We spend a lot of our time talking about the same things. It's getting a bit boring.

_____

3   My dad embarrasses me sometimes, but I guess all dads do.

_____

4   I don't know what May said, but I enjoyed your party.

_____

5   Miss Holloway's great, but she talks a lot.

_____

6   I've hardly got any money left. We bought a lot of things today.

_____

7   I miss my mum when she travels abroad for work.

_____

GET IT RIGHT!

so and such

Learners often confuse *so* and *such*.

✓   We had no idea that we were going to become **such** good friends.

✗   We had no idea that we were going to become *so* good friends.

✓   Luke's parents aren't **so** strict.

✗   Luke's parents aren't *such* strict.

Find and correct four mistakes.

Bringing up children is not an easy job and some parents can be such strict that their children sometimes rebel. There is so a lot of advice out there about raising children that it's not always easy to make the right decisions. Amy Chua's book was such interesting I read it twice and it contained so many useful pieces of advice. Childhood is so a significant time in your life and it's so important to get things right.

VOCABULARY

Costumes and uniforms → SB p.32

1 ⭐☆☆ **Put the letters in order to make words about costumes and uniforms. Then match the words and the pictures.**

1 giw _____
2 kelnsor _____
3 earthbob _____
4 mehtle _____
5 words _____
6 smak _____
7 delish _____
8 conhop _____
9 napor _____
10 ralheet kejcat _____
11 loftloab pot _____

A ☐ B ☐ C ☐ D ☐

E ☐ F ☐ G ☐ H ☐

I ☐ J ☐ K ☐

2 ⭐⭐☆ **Complete the story with words from Exercise 1.**

An invitation to a fancy-dress party. Cool! What was I going to wear? I thought about going as a chef but Dad's ¹_____ was filthy and I didn't have enough time to wash it. What about a knight? I could use a stick as a ²_____ and a dustbin lid as a ³_____ , but what about a ⁴_____ to wear on my head? No, a knight was too difficult. Maybe I could be a deep-sea diver and wear a ⁵_____ and use my ⁶_____ keep me warm at the party? No, it was too cold for swimwear. Then I thought about wearing my ⁷_____ and going as my favourite footballer. Not bad, but I wear that every Saturday so it's a bit boring. Then I had a brilliant idea … I arrived at Mike's house and knocked on the door. I was a rock star and I looked cool! I had long black hair, thanks to a ⁸_____ and my dad's ⁹_____ .

Bringing up children → SB p.35

3 ⭐☆☆ **Match the phrases and the definitions.**

1 do well ☐
2 strict ☐
3 do your best ☐
4 bring up ☐
5 soft ☐
6 childhood ☐
7 grow up ☐
8 get ahead in life ☐

a to try your hardest
b to raise (children)
c to describe a parent who doesn't impose a lot of rules on their children
d to be successful
e to get older
f to describe a parent who imposes a lot of rules on their children
g to make good progress at school, in your job, etc.
h the period of your life until the age of 18

4 ⭐⭐☆ **Choose the correct options.**

1 All parents want to help their children *get ahead in life / grow up*.
2 It doesn't matter if you win or lose, as long as you *do well / do your best*.
3 I had a really happy *childhood / bring up*.
4 It was difficult for my dad *growing / bringing* up three children on his own.
5 She *did / made* really well in her final exam.
6 They can do whatever they want. Their parents are really *soft / strict*.
7 My little cousin is *growing / bringing* up really quickly.
8 My parents are so *soft / strict*. They don't let me do anything.

REFERENCE
Costumes and uniforms

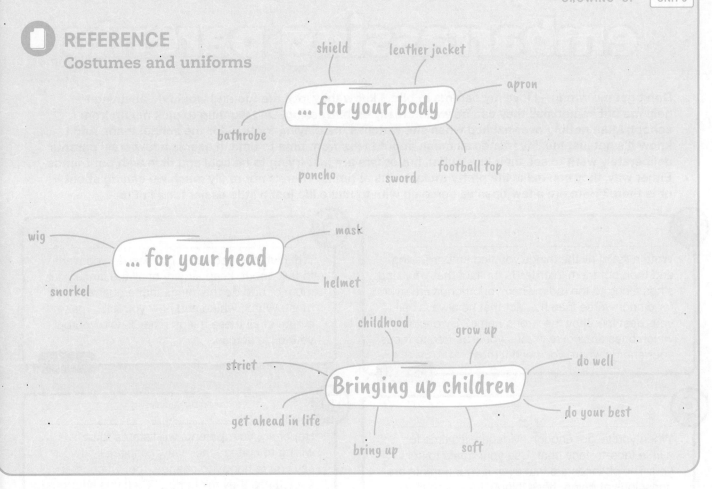

shield   leather jacket

apron

... for your body

bathrobe

poncho   sword   football top

wig   mask

... for your head

snorkel   helmet

childhood   grow up

strict   do well

Bringing up children

get ahead in life   do your best

bring up   soft

VOCABULARY EXTRA

1 Match the words and the definitions.

childcare | childproof | curfew | ground | home school | spoil

1 _____ = to allow a child to have everything that it wants, usually so that this is seen as normal by the child

2 _____ = to refuse to allow a child or young person from going out as a punishment

3 _____ = care for children provided by the government, an organisation or a person while parents are at work or are absent

4 _____ = to teach a child at home rather than sending them to school

5 _____ = difficult for children to open or use

6 _____ = a time by which a teenager must be home in the evening

2 Match the words in Exercise 1 and the pictures.

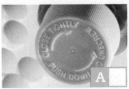 A
 B
 C
 D
 E
 F

3 Complete the opinions with words from Exercise 1. Do you agree? Why / Why not? Think of reasons.

1 'There's no point in _____ containers or bottles. Children need to learn about dangers. By making mistakes.'

2 'Parents should _____ their children when they don't do well in exams.'

3 'A _____ will keep teenagers out of trouble and help parents to worry less.'

4 'Parents who _____ a child affect their children in a negative way.'

5 'Parents and grandparents should look after young children. The children shouldn't be in _____.'

6 'Children need to go to a real school and can't learn when you _____ them.'

How to survive ...
embarrassing parents

Don't get me wrong – I love my parents to bits. I know they love me too and would do anything to help me but sometimes they can be well … really embarrassing. Dad wanting to pick me up from school, Mum getting over-excited when she watches me playing football for the school team. And I know it's not just me. My friends all moan about theirs from time to time. It seems a few cruel parents deliberately want to see their kids suffer, but others are just trying to be cool and fit in with our friends. Either way, they can make life pretty tricky for us at times. There's not really much we can do about it, or is there? Here are a few tips I've come up with to make life just a little easier for all of us.

A

Write a list of all the things you find embarrassing and then put them in order. Is the fact that your dad sings along to the radio when your friends are over for dinner worse than the fact that he always calls your best friend by the wrong name? By deciding which ones are worse means you'll be free to focus your energy where you need it most.

🔁2 👍12

B

When you've decided which issues you want to talk about, keep a diary of all the times your mum or dad do the things that embarrass you most. When, where and how you felt – make a note of all these things. They'll help you put your case across.

🔁3 👍18

C

When you've got enough evidence, it's time for a little face-to-face chat. Use your notes to help you. The chances are that even if your parents are conscious of doing these things, they probably don't realise how embarrassing they are. Keep calm. Let them know how you feel and why. Let them have their say – they'll probably want to defend themselves. Of course, you'll also have to be prepared to listen to some of the things that they're not so keen on about your behaviour. It's part of the deal. Maybe you can both agree to think more carefully about some of your actions.

🔁5 👍16

D

Hopefully, your parents will listen and be willing to change their ways, especially if you say you're happy to change, too. Of course, sometimes they might not. When this happens then the best advice I can offer is to ignore it and get on with your life. If you do this, things will be a lot easier. Remember that they once had their own embarrassing parents and the chances are many of us will be embarrassing parents ourselves one day. Maybe we shouldn't be too hard on them.

🔁1 👍35

 READING

1 **Read the magazine article. Who is it written by?**

1 a parent with a difficult teen at home

2 a young person with a difficult problem

3 someone who understands typical teenage issues

2 **Match the titles and the paragraphs in the article. There are two extra titles.**

1 Try and be more understanding

2 Don't get too upset

3 Collect the evidence

4 They don't even know why they do it

5 Choose the behaviour you find most embarrassing

6 Have a family meeting

3 CRITICAL THINKING **Read problem 1 and solutions A–C. Which solution do you think is the best? Why? Give reasons. Then read problem 2 and write your own solution.**

Problem 1: My parents make me go to bed at 9.30 pm during the week.

A What's wrong with that? Teenagers need lots of sleep. When I was young, I went to bed even earlier than that.

B Just tell them you don't agree with their decision and you're going to go to bed when you feel like it. What can they do?

C Explain that most of your friends go to bed later than you. Discuss the issue with them. Suggest a slightly later time that you can review after a week.

Problem 2: My parents are always on their phones, but they ground me when I use mine too much.

4 **Write a short paragraph (60–80 words) with your own idea about how to survive embarrassing parents.**

DEVELOPING *Writing*

An essay about the role of grandparents

1 INPUT **Read the essay and answer the questions.**

1 Why does the writer think grandparents are more active in their grandchildren's lives these days?

_____

2 Why can this be a good thing?

_____

3 What should parents be careful about?

_____

Grandparents can play an important part in children's lives. Do you agree?

Because of the high costs of professional child care, more parents in the UK are relying on their own mothers and fathers to look after their children so that they can go back to work. This means that these grandparents are getting to spend far more time with their grandchildren than their own parents did, but is this always a good thing?

Of course, grandparents can be a wonderful influence on a child's life. No one, except for their own parents, can love them more and the children will generally be well cared for. The time and attention that the child receives will help them grow up securely, knowing that they are special. This relationship often continues in later years and many teenagers have a close bond with their grandparents, knowing that they can turn to them with problems they won't always want to share with their parents.

But parents shouldn't abuse this situation. Parents should always be the most important influence in any child's life. They need to be there and make the important decisions rather than rely upon their own mothers and fathers to do so for them.

To sum up, children who grow up having a close relationship with their grandparents are very lucky indeed. However, their parents must be careful not to forget their own responsibility for their child's upbringing and happiness.

2 ANALYSE **Complete the sentences from the essay. Then check in the essay. What effect do these words have on the sentences?**

1 This means that these grandparents are getting to spend _____ more time with their grandchildren than their own parents did.

2 _____ , grandparents can be a wonderful influence in a child's life.

3 Parents should _____ be the most important influence in any child's life.

4 To sum up, children who grow up having a close relationship with their grandparents are very lucky _____ .

3 Make these sentences more emphatic using the missing words from Exercise 2.

1 You must think of the child's safety.

_____

2 It's more difficult to spend all day looking after young children.

_____

3 Grandparents love their grandchildren very much.

_____

4 Grandparents want to help their own children.

_____

4 PLAN **Make notes on these questions.**

1 What is the role of grandparents in your society?

2 What is good about the situation?

3 Is there anything to be careful about?

4 What are your thoughts?

5 PRODUCE **Do you agree that grandparents can play an important part in children's lives? Write your answer (200–250 words). Use your notes in Exercise 4. Make sure you include all the points in the checklist.**

 CHECKLIST

Include an attention-grabbing introduction.

Organise your ideas in a logical sequence.

Include examples of emphatic language.

Read through your essay to check for mistakes.

🎧 LISTENING

1 🔊 3.01 **Listen and choose the correct picture for each dialogue.**

1
 A
 B

2
 A
 B

3
 A
 B

2 🔊 3.01 **Listen again and mark the sentences T (true) or F (false).**

1 Jack doesn't recognise Emma in the photo. ☐
2 Emma has always had long hair. ☐
3 Gabi wasn't at Dan's 5th birthday party. ☐
4 Dan doesn't have his fancy dress costume any more. ☐
5 Sophie didn't learn anything new at the circus skills club. ☐
6 Matt doesn't want to be a chef now. ☐

3 🔊 3.01 **Make the sentences more emphatic using the correct form of *do*, *so* or *such*. Listen to the dialogue again and check.**

1 I have long hair.
_____

2 I can see you look almost the same.
_____

3 We know how to embarrass ourselves.
_____

4 You look cute in that photo.
_____

5 You'd make a good chef.
_____

DIALOGUE

1 **Put the sentences in order to make a dialogue.**

☐ **Dad** Well it's our house and we like to keep it just a little bit tidy.

☐ **Dad** It's your bedroom. It's such a mess. Again.

☐ **Dad** Because maybe when I go to check your room in half an hour, it will be perfect.

☐ **Dad** Very funny, Josh. Now I did say that if your room was a mess, I would ground you for a week.

☐ **Dad** You do know how to annoy your mum, Josh.

☐ **Dad** I can, but maybe I won't need to.

☐ **Josh** It will be, Dad. Thanks for the second chance.

☐ **Josh** Well, it's my bedroom so I don't see what the problem is.

☐ **Josh** Why not?

☐ **Josh** A bit tidy? This house is so tidy, we could invite anyone round for dinner now.

☐ **Josh** What have I done now?

☐ **Josh** No way, Dad, you can't do that. I can't stay here without seeing my friends for a whole week.

2 **Make the sentences more emphatic using the words in brackets.**

Mum Why didn't you clean your room?

Jay But I cleaned it, Mum. (did)
¹_____

Mum Really? Last time I looked it was a mess. (such)
²_____

Jay When was that?

Mum Five minutes ago!

Jay Well go and have a look now. It's tidy, you won't believe it. (so)
³_____

Mum And if I look under the bed?

Jay Mum, you know how to be annoying, don't you? Just give me five more minutes then.

3 **Write a short dialogue between a parent and child (6–10 lines). Use at least two examples of emphatic language.**

PRONUNCIATION
Adding emphasis **Go to page 118.** 🎧

LISTENING
Part 3: Multiple matching

1 🔊 3.03 **You will hear five short extracts in which people are talking about family holidays. For questions 1–5, choose from the list (A–H) what each speaker says about them. Use the letters only once. There are three extra letters which you do not need to use.**

A They're never as good as I hope they will be.

B They're usually very stressful.

C Everyone does what they want to do.

D My parents worry too much about showing us a good time.

E It's an opportunity to spend quality time with everyone.

F We can never really relax on them.

G We never go to places that I want to go to.

H I think I've become too grown-up for them.

Speaker 1 ☐
Speaker 2 ☐
Speaker 3 ☐
Speaker 4 ☐
Speaker 5 ☐

EXAM GUIDE

In this part of the exam you see eight options which contain ideas and information from the audio. You need to match these options to the speaker for which they are the most accurate detail or main point of what they have said / what they believe.

You hear five different people talking about five different experiences around the same subject. You hear each extract twice.

On the exam paper there are eight options to choose from. Your job is to match one to each of the speakers. There are three options you won't use.

Before you listen, read through the options to prepare yourself for the sorts of things you will hear.

You will need to listen out for attitudes, opinions, purpose, feelings, main points and details.

Listen to each speaker carefully. You will sometimes hear information that seems to relate to more than one option – listen carefully to be sure the meaning matches the wording of the option exactly.

Use your second listening to confirm answers you have already chosen and answer those questions you weren't able to the first time round.

© GRAMMAR

*be/get used to (doing)
vs. used to (do)*

 → SB p.40

1 ★☆☆ **Complete with the correct infinitive or gerund form of the verb.**

1 That supermarket used to _____ a cinema. (be)
2 When I first started my Saturday job, I couldn't get used to _____ early. (get up)
3 My mother has finally got used to _____ video calls to us. (make)
4 João comes from Brazil, so he isn't used to _____ British food yet. (eat)
5 Lucy used to _____ jeans all the time when she was a student. (wear)
6 We live near the park and we're used to _____ there every day. (go)
7 I wonder if I'll ever get used to _____ away from home. (live)
8 When we visited Mexico City, we weren't used to _____ in so much traffic. (drive)

2 ★★☆ **Circle the correct options.**

When I was young I ¹*used to / got used to* play outside with my friends. My mum ²*used to / was used to* me going out to ride my bike with them. Sometimes I was out for hours, but she ³*used to / got used to* that, too. We often rode on mud tracks that ⁴*used to / were used to* be used by motorcyclists and they were often wet and slippery, so I ⁵*used to / got used to* falling off my bike a lot. My mum ⁶*used to / was used to* seeing me covered with mud and bruises. Now I ⁷*used to / am used to* driving safely in my car and staying clean! I don't think I could ⁸*be used to / get used to* riding a bike again now.

3 ★★☆ **Complete the sentences with the correct form of *be* or *get*.**

1 Julia is Mexican so she _____ used to hot weather.
2 My uncle's working in Berlin, so he's _____ used to speaking German.
3 It never takes me long to _____ used to being in another country.
4 My father lived in Italy for years, but he never _____ used to driving on the right.
5 My grandmother _____ used to living in her small flat now, and she's very happy.
6 Kasper grew up in Norway. As a child he _____ used to skiing to school.
7 I love warm weather. I could never _____ used to living in a cold country.
8 People in some parts of the world _____ used to experiencing earthquakes.
9 On holiday, I went to the beach every day. That's something I could easily _____ used to doing!

4 ★★★ **Complete the sentences so that they are true for you.**

1 When I was younger, I used to
_____

2 When I started school it wasn't easy to get used to
_____

3 Now I am used to
_____

4 My best friend was used to
_____
before I met him/her.

5 My parents have never got used to
_____

Adverbs and adverbial phrases → SB p.43

5 ★☆☆ **Complete the sentences with the adverb form of the adjective in brackets.**

0 The students completed all the exercises
_____easily_____ . (easy)

1 The car was going too _____ for the
police to catch up with. (fast)

2 The singer sang the song _____ .
(beautiful)

3 Matty didn't feel _____ enough to go to
school yesterday. (good)

4 My eyes _____ became accustomed to
the dark. (slow)

5 Sam worked really _____ to finish the job
on time. (hard)

6 ★☆☆ **Complete the sentences with the words
in the list.**

> different | enjoyable | excitement | fear
> friendly | interest | strange | surprise

1 We really like Ms Philips, who teaches PE in an
_____ way.

2 We all jumped with _____ when the
door slammed.

3 She came second, but she congratulated the winner
in a _____ way.

4 The fans screamed with _____ when the
band walked onto the stage.

5 Nobody understood the question, until the teacher
explained it in a _____ way.

6 Fran started to shake with _____ when
she looked over the edge of the cliff.

7 I was walking in a _____ way because I
had hurt my foot.

8 Harry told us a long, boring story which we listened
to without much _____ .

7 ★★★ **Complete the sentences so that they are
true for you.**

1 I watch _____ on TV
_____

2 I do my homework _____

3 I read books _____

4 I always try to _____ in a
friendly way.

5 I like to _____ in a different way.

6 I admire people who _____
without fear.

7 I know someone who walks
_____

8 I go to the maths class _____

8 ★★★ **Write complete sentences from the
prompts using adverbial phrases.**

0 Maria / ask / her hairdresser / style / her hair /
different
Maria asked her hairdresser to style her hair in a
different way.

1 Jack / approach / lion / fear
_____

2 Freya / carry / three suitcases / difficulty
_____

3 The boys / eat / burgers / enthusiasm
_____

4 Greg / ride / horse / awkward
_____

5 Elena / watch / football match / interest
_____

GET IT *RIGHT!*

Adverbs

Learners often make word order errors with adverbs.

✓ You can **easily find** a hotel.

✗ You can find easily a hotel.

Put the words in order to make sentences.

1 finish / by / I'll / project / next / definitely / the /
Monday
_____

2 immediately / you / It's / thing / good / that /
came / a
_____

3 your / I / view / understand / point / totally / of
_____

4 and / Dan / on / hard / his / got / worked / top /
homework / marks
_____

5 Jo and Kate / would / hear / quietly / so / speaking /
no one / were / them
_____

6 job / creatively / to / in / Do / always / think / have /
your / you / ?
_____

7 locally / so / I / home / walk / live / I / can
_____

8 eaten / probably / pizza / the / This / I've / is / best /
ever
_____

VOCABULARY
Personality adjectives → SB p.40

1 ★★☆ **Complete the puzzle. Read what each person says and write the adjective to describe the person. Find the mystery word.**

```
        1 ☐☐☐☐☐☐☐
      2 ☐☐☐☐☐☐☐☐☐☐
    3 ☐☐☐☐☐☐☐☐☐
          4 ☐☐☐☐☐☐☐☐☐
      5 ☐☐☐☐☐☐☐☐
  6 ☐☐☐☐☐☐
        7 ☐☐☐☐☐☐☐☐☐
  8 ☐☐☐☐☐☐
  9 ☐☐☐☐☐☐☐☐
```

1 'I learn quickly and easily.'
2 'I get lots of new ideas.'
3 'If I say I'll do something, then I do it.'
4 'I'm the best, by far!'
5 'I always think carefully before I do anything.'
6 'I'm sure of my abilities.'
7 'I don't sit around thinking for a long time.'
8 'I know where everything is.'
9 'I'm better at doing things than thinking about things.'

Mystery word: 'I want it – and I want it now!'

2 ★★☆ **Complete the dialogues with appropriate adjectives.**

1 A She gets angry at everything I say.
  B Oh, I know, she's quite _____ .
2 A He drives quite slowly.
  B Yes, he's a _____ driver, usually.
3 A She designs such different, interesting things!
  B Yes, she's very _____ .
4 A Let's go to Australia for our holiday.
  B Oh, be _____ . We haven't got enough money for that.
5 A Do you think she'll do what she promised?
  B Oh yes – she's very _____ .
6 A She thinks she's the best. I guess she's confident.
  B No, it's more than that – she's really _____ .
7 A Hurry up!
  B OK. Don't be so _____ !
8 A He isn't very interesting, is he?
  B No, he's a bit _____ , really.

Common adverbial phrases → SB p.43

3 ★☆☆ **Complete the sentences with the phrases in the list.**

by accident	in a hurry
in a panic	in a row	in private
in public	in secret	on purpose

1 Sorry, I can't stop and talk now – I'm _____ .
2 I made a mistake – I clicked the wrong button and deleted the file _____ .
3 I'm a nervous person – I don't think I could ever make a speech _____ .
4 Has any country ever won the World Cup three times _____ ?
5 I only ever sing _____ – in the shower, for example.
6 I didn't know you all met in town at the weekend. Why did you meet _____ without telling me?
7 I was so worried about being late that I started to do everything _____ .
8 I'm sorry I broke it, but I promise you, I didn't do it _____ !

WordWise → SB p.41
Expressions with *good*

4 ★★☆ **Use phrases with *good* to complete the sentences.**

0 She isn't going to Australia just for a holiday – she's going there ___*for good*___ .
1 Oh, no! This food is awful! Well, I guess I'm _____ at cooking.
2 A It's really cold today.
  B Yes. _____ we're wearing our coats.
3 A How are you getting on?
  B _____ . I think I'll finish in ten minutes.
4 I've apologised to her three times, but _____ – she's still angry with me.

5 ★★★ **Complete the sentences so that they are true for you.**

1 I'm not very good at _____ _____ .
2 It's a good thing that I _____ _____ .
3 I'm going to _____ _____ for good.
4 I would really like to _____ , but it's no good.

REFERENCE

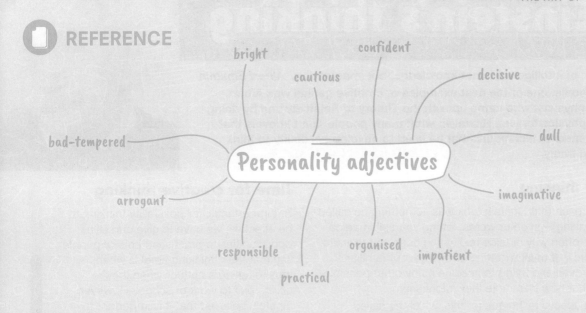

COMMON ADVERBIAL PHRASES

by accident	in a row	in secret
in a hurry	in private	on purpose
in a panic	in public	

GOOD

for good	not very good at
it's a good thing	so far, so good
it's no good	

VOCABULARY EXTRA

1 Match the adverbial phrases and the adverbs.

> all of a sudden | before long | by far | without a sound | without warning

0 suddenly: _____*all of a sudden*_____

1 silently: _____

2 much better (or worse) than anything else: _____

3 unexpectedly: _____

4 soon: _____

2 Choose the correct adverbial phrases.

1 We went into the house without *warning / a sound* because it was late and everyone was asleep.

2 Don't worry. We'll get our exam results *all of a sudden / before long*. I'm sure you've passed.

3 This is the highest mountain we've climbed *by far / all of a sudden*.

4 The government closed all the shops in the town *before long / without warning*.

5 We were walking along the street when *all of a sudden / by far*, a horse appeared.

3 Write a short story (100–120 words). Choose one of the sentences below to start your story.

1 I was sitting in my bedroom when all of a sudden …

2 I crept down the stairs without a sound and …

3 Before long, I'll …

4 The hardest decision I've ever made by far was when I …

5 I was walking home from school one day last week when without warning …

Einstein's thinking

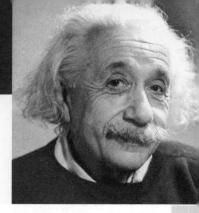

'The true sign of intelligence is not knowledge, but imagination.' *Albert Einstein*
For a lot of people, one of the best examples of creative genius was Albert Einstein, the physicist who came up with the Theory of Relativity and by doing so, changed physics forever. However, what many people don't know is that Einstein had specific techniques that he used to develop his ability to think creatively and freely.

Possibility thinking

The main approach that Einstein took was something he called 'possibility thinking' – in other words, letting yourself imagine things that are often way outside reality and pushing the limits of what you know. It means getting away from our familiar thoughts and ideas and trying to imagine many other possible things, no matter how incredible they might seem.

Einstein had a special technique for this, which he called 'the thought experiment'. This example of possibility thinking is simply an experiment that you do inside your own head. Perhaps the most famous thought experiment is the one that Einstein says he used to get himself on the path towards the Theory of Relativity. Einstein was interested in light, the speed of light and its relationship to time, so what he did was to imagine himself riding on a beam of sunlight. Now, that's an impossible thing to do, of course, but Einstein said that using his imagination like this allowed him to understand some of the relationships between light and time, and how they work.

Essentially, how we experience time depends on where we are and what we are doing. Einstein explained it as follows: 'When you're talking to a pretty girl, an hour seems like a minute. If you sit on a hot fire, a minute seems like an hour. That's relativity.'

Time for creative thinking

But importantly, for possibility thinking to be effective, we have to give ourselves opportunities to practise it. Lots of people say that their 'thinking time' is when they're taking a bath or when they're on the bus to work or school. However, Einstein believed that it is important to devote a period of time every day to 'creative thinking': whatever problem or idea it is that interests you, set aside some time every day to thinking about it – concentrated thinking. And he was a great believer in images, too. He said that he often thought 'in a stream of pictures' and that this was a powerful way to think.

Einstein also believed in thinking about a problem for a long time and not giving up. As he once said, 'I think and think for months and years; 99 times, the conclusion is false. The 100th time, I am right.'

READING

1   Read the article. Write three types of thinking that Einstein believed were important.

_____

_____

_____

2   Read the article again. Match the parts of the sentences.

   1   Einstein is known as the genius who ☐
   2   Not everybody knows that Einstein ☐
   3   Possibility thinking means ☐
   4   Einstein came up with an image ☐
   5   The image helped him ☐
   6   Possibility thinking only really works ☐
   7   Einstein felt that thinking in pictures ☐
   8   Einstein thought it was important ☐

   a   develop his Theory of Relativity.
   b   to keep thinking until you get the answer.
   c   first thought of the Theory of Relativity.
   d   had things that he did to help him think freely.
   e   was something very powerful.
   f   of himself travelling on a beam of light.
   g   moving away from the ways that we usually think.
   h   if we practise it regularly.

3   CRITICAL THINKING   Read the problems below. Which type of thinking do you need to solve them: possibility or creative?

   1   Look at the puzzle. Connect the dots using only four lines.
      _____

   2   Is this a banana or a telephone?
      _____

   3   Farmer Brown wants to cross the river with his goat and a cabbage, but he also has to take a wolf. How can he take the animals and the cabbage across without the wolf eating the goat and the goat eating the cabbage? _____

4   Solve the problems in Exercise 3.

5   When and where are you able to think the most freely? Write a short paragraph (80–100 words).

PRONUNCIATION
Pronouncing words with *gh* Go to page 119.

DEVELOPING Writing

Writing an email of advice

1 **INPUT** **Read Marnie's email. What does she want her sister Becca to do?**

> ⭐ **Marnie**
> Marnie@thinkmail.com
>
> Hi Becca,
> **[A]** How are things with you? How's it going at university? I hope you're enjoying everything and not working too hard!
> **[B]** Well, <u>you know that</u> I'm going to be doing my end-of-year exams soon, right? Just like you did all those years ago. <u>Well</u>, I'm writing to ask you for some advice. <u>The thing is</u>, I just can't get going with revision, because I'm really busy with lots of things at school and at home. <u>Now</u>, I know that revision's really, really important, but I'm finding that days are going past and I'm not fitting it in. It's really frustrating. I try to organise my time, but it's hopeless! I'm just useless at it. I also don't really have any techniques for it and I think I'll never come up with anything.
> **[C]** Have you got any tips you can give me?
> **[D]** Now, I know you're busy too, but I'm hoping you can find a few minutes to help your sweet younger sister out! The thing is, I don't know who else to ask.
> See you soon, I hope!
> Love,
> Marnie.

2 **Match the underlined phrases in the email with the definitions.**

1 We use this phrase to introduce our main concern or problem. _____

2 We use this phrase to start talking about something the reader/listener already knows. _____

3 We use this word to give emphasis to what we are about to say. _____

4 We use this word to signal we're going to talk about something important. _____

3 **Complete the sentences with the underlined phrases in the email.**

1 Martha – _____ there's a test tomorrow, right?

2 I'd like to give you some advice, but _____ , I'm no good at revision myself!

3 So why am I writing? _____ , because you asked for my advice, of course!

4 _____ , you might not like all these ideas, but I'm going to send them anyway.

4 **ANALYSE** **Match the information (1–4) with the paragraphs (A–D).**

1 The main body of the email – the problem. ☐

2 Explaining that you don't want to cause the person a lot of problems and why you're writing. ☐

3 Saying what you want the reader to do. ☐

4 Some personal exchange about the other person's life. ☐

5 **PLAN** **Read the ideas of how to help Marnie. Add two more ideas. Cross through any that you don't like.**

Revise early in the day – it's better than at night.

Make a timetable for every day. Tell other people when you're going to do revision.

Ask someone to test you as soon as you've done some revision.

Make sure to be away from computers, laptops, tablets, etc. when you revise.

Put revision notes around the house so you keep seeing them.

Keep as healthy as you can.

_____

_____

6 **PRODUCE** **Imagine you are Becca. Write your reply to Marnie (150–200 words). Use your ideas in Exercise 5. Make sure you include all the points in the checklist.**

✓ **CHECKLIST**

☐ Use a structure for an email.

☐ Include some personal exchanges in your introduction.

☐ Use expressions from Exercise 3.

☐ Give the most useful advice and say why.

☐ Close the email in a friendly way, e.g. *Good luck! / I'm sure you'll do great. / I hope this is helpful.*

1 🔊 4.03 **Listen and write the number of the dialogue next to the correct picture.**

2 🔊 4.03 **Listen again and complete the summaries with between one and three words in each gap.**

1 Tom is trying to ¹_____
a signal, but he can't. They want to get to the
²_____ .
Daisy offers to help, but Tom decides to try again.
Then he begins to ³_____ ,
so Daisy tells him to calm down.
Daisy then tries but she can't
⁴_____ either.
Daisy has an idea and she decides
to ⁵_____ or
⁶_____ . Tom think Daisy's idea
is great.

2 Billy asks his friend Megan for her opinion
about his painting. She says it isn't
⁷_____ his last one. Then
she admits that ⁸_____
that good. Billy says that he's going to
⁹_____ painting, but Megan
tries to persuade him not to. Billy says that he will
¹⁰_____ photography. He never
wants to ¹¹_____ paints and
brushes again.

3 Gemma and her friends need to find a way to
¹²_____ the first puzzle
in the Escape Room. They've already been in
the room for ¹³_____ , but
they're stuck. Gemma's worried because she
¹⁴_____ stay in the room until
the end. Aiden thinks they might have to take a
¹⁵_____ . He suggests using
¹⁶_____ thinking. While he is
talking to Gemma, Luke has found the answer and
solved the first puzzle.

DIALOGUE

1 **Put the sentences in order to make dialogues.**

1 ☐ **Nina** I'm doing a crossword puzzle and I've only got three answers left to find.

☐ **Nina** This is so frustrating!

☐ **Nina** No chance! I can't give up like that. That would be cheating.

☐ **Nina** Oh, that's OK. I always prefer to do them on my own, anyway. But I'm really stuck right now.

☐ **Marcus** A crossword? I'm no good at those. I can't help you, I'm afraid.

☐ **Marcus** OK then. Well, good luck, tell me when you've finished it!

☐ **Marcus** What is it? What are you trying to do?

☐ **Marcus** Well, if you're stuck, why don't you just look at the answers? No one will know!

2 ☐ **Ella** Yes, I am. Well, I'm trying to. But to be honest, I can't do it.

☐ **Ella** Oh, don't be like that. You're good at these things, usually.

☐ **Ella** Hello? Jamie, is that you?

☐ **Ella** Well, now I give up. I was hoping you might help me! That's why I called.

☐ **Jamie** I know I am. That's why I'm so frustrated. I've tried everything, but it's hopeless.

☐ **Jamie** Hi, Ella. How are you? Are you doing the homework?

☐ **Jamie** I'm stuck, too. I'll never get it right, I'm sure.

☐ **Jamie** Sorry, but there you go. I'll see you tomorrow, Ella. Bye.

PHRASES FOR FLUENCY   → SB p.44

1 **Circle the correct options.**

1 **A** This is terrible. I'm starting to panic!
   B OK, *just calm down / you can't be serious*, it'll be OK.

2 **A** Your hair looks awful!
   B You know, *you're really out of order / that's just it* when you say things like that.

3 **A** It's so difficult to find a good babysitter these days.
   B *That's just it / Give it a rest*, no one's available at short notice!

4 **A** Come on, write it down.
   B Sorry, but how do you spell it *off / again*?

5 **A** Honestly – my dad was an international footballer!
   B Oh, *calm down / give it a rest*!

6 **A** I'm going for a swim in the sea.
   B But it's freezing! *You're out of order / You can't be serious*!

B2 First for Schools

EXAM GUIDE: WRITING AN ESSAY

In this part of the exam, you have to write an essay. You will have two ideas for the essay and you can choose your own idea. Make sure you have a clear structure for your essay and organise the information. You have to include three points and two of those points are given. You must think of your own point for the third one.

- Introduction: Explain what the title means according to you and include your opinion.
- Paragraph 2: Include the first point. Start with a topic sentence and add reasons or examples.
- Paragraph 3: Include the second point. Start with a topic sentence and add reasons or examples.
- Paragraph 4: Include your own point. Start with a topic sentence and add reasons or examples.
- Conclusion: Summarise the essay in one sentence restate your opinion.

In your English class you have been talking about travel and tourism. Now your English teacher has asked you to write an essay.

Write an essay using all the notes and give reasons for your point of view.

Tourism is causing problems for a lot of countries but a lot of countries need tourism to survive. Do you agree? Write 140–190 words in an appropriate style.

Notes
Write about:
1. the economic benefits of tourism
2. the negative effects of tourism
3. _____ (your own idea)

1 **Read Harry's essay and answer the questions.**

1 Does he answer the essay question?
_____

2 Does he agree or disagree?
_____

3 Which idea of his own did Harry add?
_____

2 **Look at the underlined words in the essay. Which ones introduce an argument? Which give an opinion?**

Today, a lot of countries need tourism because it generates a lot of income. In my opinion, tourism can cause problems, but tourism is necessary.

One of the main advantages for tourism is that it helps a country's economy and provides jobs for local people. First of all, tourists spend a lot of money when they travel, on accommodation, transport, food, souvenirs and tours. This gives extra income to a country's economy. Secondly, tourism provides more jobs in certain areas like cafés and restaurants, tour guides, hotel staff and shop owners. It is also important to note that, without tourism, people who work in these industries may not have jobs.

On the other hand, tourism can have a negative effect on countries by damaging popular tourist attractions because so many tourists visit them at the same time. However, some sights like Machu Picchu manage this by only allowing a certain number of tourists to visit each day.

Tourism also means travel. When people travel, they can learn about other countries, their culture and language. These are important life skills and can lead to a more tolerant society because we can see things from a different point of view.

In conclusion, I believe that although tourism has certain negative effects on the environment, it has a positive effect on a country's economy and provides jobs for a lot of local people. To my mind, the benefits outweigh the drawbacks.

3 **Write an essay of your own. Choose the same task as Harry or the task below.**

Air travel should be banned because it causes serious environmental problems. Do you agree? Write 140–190 words in an appropriate style.

Notes
Write about:
1. the negative impact of air travel on the environment
2. the economic impact of banning air travel
3. _____ (your own idea)

CONSOLIDATION

🎧 LISTENING

1 🔊 **4.04** **Listen to Paul talking about his childhood and circle the correct options.**

1 Who used to argue the most in his family home?
   A Paul with his parents.
   B Paul with his sister and brother.
   C Paul's mum with his dad.

2 What did Paul think was great about how his parents raised him?
   A They weren't very strict with him.
   B They always had clear expectations.
   C They were always happy to play board games.

3 How did they treat his friends?
   A They weren't very friendly.
   B They were too interfering with them.
   C They wanted to know about them as people.

2 🔊 **4.04** **Listen again and mark the sentences T (true) or F (false).**

1 Paul doesn't remember his parents ever fighting. ☐

2 Paul thinks his parents were too strict at times. ☐

3 Paul couldn't join in with some of the conversations in the school playground. ☐

4 Paul's parents encouraged him to be active. ☐

5 Paul's dad would sometimes embarrass him. ☐

⊚ GRAMMAR

3 **Put the words in order to make sentences.**

1 own / The / of / tablet / friends / vast / my / majority / have / their
   _____

2 board game / We / enough / tonight / players / got / for / haven't / the
   _____

3 that / so / fix / practical / he / anything / He / can / is
   _____

4 to / I / do / do / listening / nothing / to / when / I've / music / enjoy / got
   _____

5 never / I'll / early / to / waking / used / up / get / so
   _____

6 teaches / White / way / chemistry / an / Mr / enjoyable / in
   _____

🔤 VOCABULARY

4 **Choose the correct answers.**

1 We didn't recognise him because he was wearing a *mask / poncho*.

2 Steve is so *arrogant / cautious*. He thinks he's better than all of us.

3 Knights carried a *shield / sword* to protect themselves from arrows.

4 Cyclists should wear *an apron / a helmet* to protect their head.

5 My dad's not very *confident / decisive*. He can never make up his mind.

6 Let's wear a pink *cape / wig* to make our hair look different at the party.

7 Don't be so *impatient / dull*. I'll be ready to go in five minutes.

8 Her teachers say she's *responsible / bright* and should do well.

5 **Match the sentences.**

1 My dad's not very strict. ☐
2 Your homework's full of silly mistakes. ☐
3 I had a really happy childhood. ☐
4 He didn't do that by accident. ☐
5 Bring your children up as well as you can. ☐
6 She's a very secretive woman. ☐
7 Our football team's doing really well. ☐
8 Always try and do your best at school. ☐

a It will help you get ahead in life.
b It will help them do well in life.
c He did it on purpose.
d She lives her life in private.
e In fact he's quite soft actually.
f They've won five games in a row now.
g I grew up with a lot of love and care.
h You did it in a hurry, didn't you?

DIALOGUE

6 Put the sentences in order to make a dialogue.

☐ **Dad** OK, calm down. You always give up too easily.

☐ **Dad** What do you mean, give up? What do you have to do?

☐ **Dad** Music and art. That sounds perfect for you.

☐ **Dad** What's the matter, Oscar?

☐ **Dad** That's a bit out of order. I'm only trying to help.

☐ **Dad** No you're not. You just need a good idea.

☐ **Oscar** I have to design a CD cover for my favourite band.

☐ **Oscar** I know. I'm sorry, Dad. Maybe I just need a bit of a break.

☐ **Oscar** That's the problem, Dad. I just can't come up with anything. It's hopeless!

☐ **Oscar** Leave it out, Dad. Just leave me alone.

☐ **Oscar** That's what I thought. But I'm useless.

☐ **Oscar** It's this school art project. I give up.

READING

7 Read the article and match the titles (1–7) with the paragraphs (A–E). There are two extra titles.

1 Time management ☐
2 Food and nutrition ☐
3 Illness and medicines ☐
4 Problem solving ☐
5 Communication ☐
6 Good manners ☐
7 Finance ☐

8 Match these ideas with the paragraphs.

1 planning how and when to spend your money ☐
2 household appliances and practical skills ☐
3 meeting deadlines ☐
4 using technology to help you learn a new skill ☐
5 the importance of being well-informed about news and current affairs ☐

WRITING

9 Write a short paragraph for the article (100–120 words). Include advice about another way to successfully 'learn to adult'.

How to adult ... successfully!

We're often in a hurry to move on to the next stage of our life. So, are you ready for your childhood to end and to become an adult? If you're not, don't panic! Just follow these five simple steps.

A _____

Plan how you are going to spend your weekly allowance. Think about different ways to spend your money. Can you buy something cheaper in a sale or from a second-hand website or shop? Make sensible choices with your money and ask yourself if something is essential or a luxury. Sometimes, you have to wait for things you want and it's much more satisfying if you've had to save for something when you do finally get it.

B _____

One day, you'll have to be responsible for your own meals, so it's a good idea to start now. Choose a recipe each week and offer to buy all the ingredients and then prepare and cook a meal for your family or friends. Cooking is a very sociable thing and it's a great skill to have. You can start with simple step-by-step recipes on cooking videos. Alternatively, you can just watch and learn from your parents.

C _____

Your parents aren't always going to be around telling you what to do and when to do something. It's a good idea to take responsibility for things yourself now. Use a calendar to make a note of deadlines and set reminders on your phone about when to do things, like school work, meeting friends or even making your own appointments. Find a way to manage your time that works for you. Don't forget to reward yourself after you've done something – watch an episode of your favourite series or get a drink from your favourite café. It's always good to have things to look forward to.

D _____

Part of being independent is thinking about how to do things when you're studying or working away from home and your parents aren't around to answer your questions or do things for you. Learn how do simple things like change a light bulb, unblock a sink, repair a puncture or use a map. Make sure you know how to iron your clothes and how a washing machine works, too!

E _____

It's never been more important to be well informed than it is just now. It's a good idea to try and listen to news and keep up-to-date with current affairs on a regular basis. Don't just read about what's going on locally. Find out about national and international news stories. Be careful to read trusted sources and make sure you can tell the difference between real news and fake news.

Grammar video

GRAMMAR
Obligation, permission
and prohibition (review) → SB p.50

1 ★☆☆ **Choose the correct options.**

1 You *don't have to / aren't supposed to* eat too many sweet things. They're bad for your teeth.

2 He *didn't let me / didn't need to* buy a new tablet. He already had one.

3 We *are not allowed to / had better* eat in the library. It's not permitted.

4 My parents *don't let me / allow me to* use my computer after 8 pm. They don't want me to spend all evening on it.

5 We *have to / don't have to* turn off our phones in school. We can't use them in class.

6 You *had better / shouldn't* spend all evening texting your friends. Do something else instead.

2 ★★☆ **Complete the sentences with the modal verbs in the list.**

> aren't allowed to | didn't let | didn't
> have to | had better made | mustn't

1 'You have to wear a hat and scarf today. It's cold.'
My mum _____ me wear a hat and scarf today.

2 'You have to get to school early tomorrow. The coach leaves at 8 am.'
I _____ be late to school tomorrow morning.

3 'You can't bring your scooter into this restaurant.'
We _____ take our scooters into the restaurant.

4 'I really need a new school jumper. This one is too small.'
I _____ buy a new jumper.

5 'You can't go to the cinema tonight.'
My dad _____ us go to the cinema last night.

6 'It wasn't necessary for Tom to lend me his tablet.'
Tom _____ lend me his tablet.

3 ★★★ **Put the words in order to complete the dialogues. Use the correct form of the verbs.**

1 A Why haven't you got your mobile phone with you today?
B mum / My / make / it / leave / me / at / home
_____

2 A Why didn't you come climbing on Saturday?
_____
B parents / My / not allow / to / me / go
_____

3 A Are you ready to go yet?
B No, I can't find my Geography homework.
A had better / You / find / it / soon
_____

4 A Why were you late yesterday?
B have to / I / my / Sorry, / bedroom / tidy
_____

5 A I gave Joanna my phone yesterday.
B must not / you / But / give / phone / your / anyone / to
_____

6 A Did you see the match last night?
B stay / it / parents / No, / up / not let / my / me / for
_____

4 ★★★ **Complete the sentences so that they are true for you. Choose from the verbs in the list and give a reason.**

> let / don't let have to / don't have to
> must / mustn't
> should / shouldn't allowed to / not allowed to

1 My parents _____ me play on the tablet as much as I want because _____

2 I _____ use my phone too much because _____

3 I _____ have a TV in my bedroom because _____

4 I _____ think carefully before I post photos of friends and family because _____

Necessity: (*didn't*) *need to / needn't have*

→ SB p.51

5 ⭐☆☆ **Match the statements and responses.**

1 The battery for my laptop has run out. ☐
2 I don't have enough space on my hard drive. ☐
3 I didn't have a European plug. ☐
4 We were late yesterday. ☐
5 I arrived an hour before the concert. ☐
6 I bought a Spanish dictionary yesterday. ☐
7 I failed my History exam. ☐
8 My friends keep texting me. I can't work. ☐

a You needn't have left home so early.
b You needed to take an earlier bus.
c I've got one. You needn't have bought one.
d You need to get a charger.
e Turn your phone off. You need to finish your homework.
f You needed to do more revision for it.
g You needed to get an adaptor.
h You need to delete some files.

6 ⭐⭐☆ **Read the situations. Then make comments with *didn't need to* or *needn't have*.**

0 I bought two concert tickets. My friend had already bought them.
   I needn't have bought the tickets.

1 Daniel didn't do his homework last night. He'd already done it the night before.
   _____

2 Sara didn't revise for her History exam. She passed it easily anyway.
   _____

3 I took a thick jumper with me yesterday, but it was a hot, sunny day.
   _____

4 Lucy cooked Josh a birthday cake, but his mum had already bought him one from the shops.
   _____

5 Liam didn't have dinner at home because he knew there was food at the party.
   _____

6 We took a taxi from the station, but the concert hall was only 200 metres away so we could have walked there.
   _____

7 I'd already messaged Louisa and that's why I didn't call her.
   _____

Ability in the past: *could, was / were able to, managed to, succeeded in doing*

→ SB p.53

7 ⭐⭐☆ **Write sentences using the prompts.**

0 I / not manage / mend / my phone / yet
   I haven't managed to mend my phone yet.

1 James / not succeed / pass / his driving test / yet
   _____

2 I / not able to / find / my charger / yet
   _____

3 Laura / not able to / swim / yesterday
   _____

4 We / succeed / climb / Ben Nevis / at the weekend
   _____

5 They / not able to / access / the internet / at home / last night
   _____

6 He / not have / much / time / but / he / manage to / finish / the project
   _____

 GET IT RIGHT!

must

Learners often use *should*, *would*, and *can* instead of *must*.

✓ I mustn't forget to give you my phone number.
✗ I shouldn't forget to give you my phone number.

Choose the correct options.

1 We *can / must / would* admit that peer pressure can be a problem.
2 They *shouldn't / can't / mustn't* be using artificial flowers – it doesn't look nice.
3 I really *can / would / must* get a new headset – this one doesn't work very well.
4 Harry *mustn't / can't / wouldn't* have arrived yet as his car isn't here.
5 Applicants *can / should / must* have cooking experience to apply for this job. Applicants without experience won't be considered.
6 *Should / Would / Must* you do that? It's very irritating!
7 The children *wouldn't / mustn't / can't* arrive home late unless there was a problem.
8 The spectators *should / must / can* have seen the man run on stage. He ran right across it!

Az VOCABULARY
Technology (nouns) → SB p.50

1 ★☆☆ **Unscramble the words and match them with the pictures.**

1 vetecitpro seac _____
2 ewmabc _____
3 gcerahr _____
4 woper dela _____
5 glup _____
6 dehates _____

A ☐ B ☐
C ☐ D ☐
E ☐ F ☐

2 ★★☆ **What do they need? Match the sentences (1–4) to the objects (a–d).**

1 ☐ *I'm connecting my camera to my laptop.*

2 ☐ *You need to include it in your email address.*

3 ☐ *What do I need to connect to the wi-fi?*

4 ☐ *You can't use a European plug here.*

a wireless router   c USB port
b adaptor   d 'at' symbol

3 ★★☆ **Read the definitions. What are they?**

1 It provides access to the internet or to a private computer network. _____
2 It stops my phone from being scratched or damaged. _____
3 It connects my laptop to the mains electricity. _____
4 It holds an earphone and a microphone in place on your head. _____
5 You can use it to video chat over the internet. _____

Technology (verbs) → SB p.51

4 ★★☆ **Complete the puzzle.**

1 My sister … updates on her blog once a week.
2 We … interviews with our favourite singers.
3 I'd better … my laptop in before the battery dies.
4 My dad usually … his phone every two years.
5 I … all of my digital photos on my memory stick.
6 You can find lots of interesting information when you … the internet.
7 I want to … music from my laptop onto my phone.
8 If you go to the café on the High Street, you can … to the wi-fi for free.

5 ★★☆ **Complete the dialogues with the correct form of the verbs in the list.**

browse | connect | post | save | stream | upgrade

1 A Have you _____ anything interesting on your blog this week?
  B No, I haven't had time.
2 A You've had the same phone for years. You should _____ it for a newer model.
  B I don't want to. I'm happy with this one.
3 A You look tired.
  B I am. I _____ the internet for hours last night.
4 A I want to watch the film awards this evening, but they're not on TV.
  B Don't worry. We can _____ it and watch it live.
5 A How do I _____ my games console to the internet?
  B You need access to a wireless connection.
6 A There isn't enough space to _____ all my music and photos on my hard drive.
  B You should store them on a cloud server.

PRONUNCIATION
The schwa sound Go to page 119. 🎧

REFERENCE

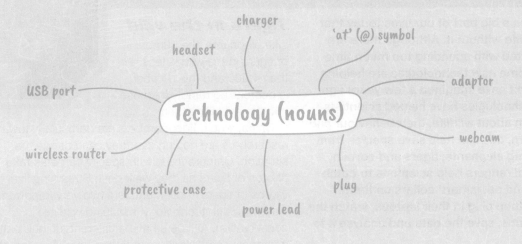

charger
headset
'at' (@) symbol
USB port
adaptor
Technology (nouns)
webcam
wireless router
protective case
plug
power lead

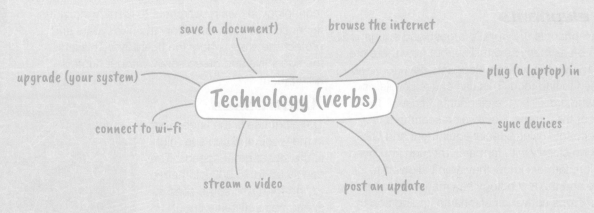

save (a document)
browse the internet
upgrade (your system)
plug (a laptop) in
Technology (verbs)
connect to wi-fi
sync devices
stream a video
post an update

VOCABULARY EXTRA

1 **Match the words and the pictures.**

> back up | bookmark | download
> receive notifications | scroll | swipe

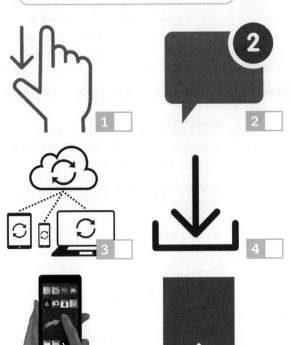

1 ☐ 2 ☐ 3 ☐ 4 ☐ 5 ☐ 6 ☐

2 **Complete the sentences with verbs from Exercise 1.**

1 What do you _____ on your phone or computer to read later?

2 Do you _____ through documents slowly or quickly to find information you need?

3 How many _____ do you _____ each day?

4 How often do you _____ new music to listen to on your phone?

5 Do you always _____ information from your phone or computer? If so, where? If not, why not?

6 Do you have to _____ across to open your phone or can you use your face or fingerprint?

3 **Answer the questions in Exercise 2.**

1 _____
2 _____
3 _____
4 _____
5 _____
6 _____

Saving lives with tech

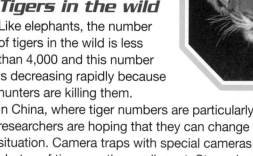

Technology is such a big part of our lives today that we can't imagine life without it. Although there are problems associated with spending too much time on our devices, some new technologies are helping in ways we couldn't have imagined a few years ago. Some of these technologies have helped scientists collect information about wildlife, their behaviour and movements. In turn, this can help save species from extinction, including elephants, tigers and certain birds. Local animal rangers help scientists to catch animals or birds and put 'smart' collars on them. Researchers can then plug in their laptops, watch the animals on webcams, save the data and analyse it to help save lives.

African elephants

The African elephant is the world's largest land animal and there used to be as many as 5 million, but now there are only about 415,000 left. African elephants have to travel huge distances to find food. This can cause problems for farmers, who are killing the elephants because they need to protect their crops. However, researchers can now track elephants using special equipment and GPS and are working closely with farmers. Through improved communication, farmers know they aren't allowed to kill the elephants and the technology has managed to help save farmers' crops as well as elephants. In addition to using smart collars, researchers have connected with people who post social-media updates about illegal activities. This is also helping them track and monitor such activities and protect more endangered species.

Tigers in the wild

Like elephants, the number of tigers in the wild is less than 4,000 and this number is decreasing rapidly because hunters are killing them.

In China, where tiger numbers are particularly low, researchers are hoping that they can change the situation. Camera traps with special cameras take photos of tigers as they walk past. Streaming live videos of tigers' movements are two very important ways in which technology is helping wildlife conservation. All tigers have a different, unique pattern of stripes – a bit like human fingerprints. The camera technology allows researchers to identify individual tigers so that they can follow them for years and protect the areas where the tigers live. This lets the tigers live and breed safely without hunters killing them.

Albatrosses

The albatross is the largest bird in the world and can soar high in the sky at great speeds. They can fly up to 15,000 kilometres to find food and some species spend years at sea without touching land. Recently, however, researchers have used GPS trackers on the birds to help them become 'police birds'. There are 22 species of albatross and eight are endangered or critically endangered. Fishing boats are also dangerous for albatrosses because some of the equipment on the boats can kill them. The researchers use the information from the birds to monitor the boats and check that they are fishing legally. As well as helping to fight illegal fishing, researchers have discovered that the birds flew over an area of more than 50 million km^2 of sea in six months. That's a long way!

📖 **READING**

1 **Read the article quickly. What do these numbers refer to?**

1 22 _____
2 4,000 _____
3 15,000 _____
4 415,000 _____
5 5 million _____
6 50 million _____

2 **Read the article again. Mark the sentences T (true), F (false), or DS (doesn't say).**

1 Technology is used to help save species. ☐
2 Researchers are not able to work with African farmers. ☐
3 All tigers have the same pattern of stripes. ☐
4 Hunters kill 150 tigers a year in China. ☐
5 An albatross can spend years flying without going on land. ☐
6 Researchers have discovered three types of fish that albatross prefer to eat. ☐

3 CRITICAL THINKING **Read the article again. Copy and complete the table with the solutions to the problems.**

Problem	Tech solution
1 Elephants eating crops; farmers killing them	
2 Hunters killing tigers	
3 Illegal fishing boats	

4 **Write a short paragraph (80–100 words) giving your opinion on technology that helps to protect and save wildlife.**

A guide to buying a phone

1 **INPUT** Read Jamie's guide to buying a phone.
Tick (✓) three things that are important to him.

1 the colour	☐	4 the camera	☐
2 the battery life	☐	5 the price	☐
3 the brand	☐		

TECH**HELP** ☰

My guide to buying a new phone

What do you look for when you buy a phone? Does your phone have to be the latest model? Does it have to look good or do you just want a phone that's easy to use and small enough to fit in your pocket? Before you buy your new phone, decide what's important to you.

First, I look at the battery life. That's very important to me. My phone must have a long battery life. It mustn't ever go flat on me. Next I look at the camera quality. I like taking photos, so I have to have a phone with a good camera. I also like to have a phone with a big screen so I can see the photos clearly. Then I look at how much memory there is because I want to make sure I have enough for photos, videos, music and all my apps and games. After that, I check the data. How much is there? How much do I need? How much does it cost to buy more? Finally, I look at the price of the contract and the phone itself. Is it affordable? I do that last, but my mum says I should do it first!

Everyone has different priorities when buying a phone, but these are the things that are important to me.

2 **ANALYSE** Read Jamie's guide again and circle the sequencing words. Then complete the list of sequencing words.

First, … _____ , …
Then, … _____ , …
Finally, …

3 **PLAN** Imagine you are going to buy one of these things: a new phone, a tablet or a laptop. Complete the mind map with your ideas.

Things that are important to me when buying a …

4 Choose five of your ideas and write them in a sequence.

First,

Next,

Then,

After that,

Finally,

5 **PRODUCE** Write your own guide to buying the thing you chose (200–250 words). Use your notes in Exercises 3 and 4. Make sure you include all the points in the checklist.

 CHECKLIST

☐ Include modal verbs in your guide.
☐ Include a variety of useful technology nouns and verbs.
☐ Put your ideas in a logical order (the most important feature first, the least important last). Use sequencing words.

1 🔊 5.02 **Listen to the radio show. Tick (✓) the correct definition.**

An influencer is a person who …

1 helps their friends shop online. ☐

2 decide which products are the most popular on social media. ☐

3 promotes things like food, fashion, health and beauty products, etc. on social media to try and influence potential buyers. ☐

2 🔊 5.02 **Listen again and choose the correct options.**

1 Daisy has … followers.
  A 200
  B 14,000
  C 100,000

2 On social media, Daisy used to …
  A post videos of her playing different sports.
  B post updates of new dance clothes.
  C post and stream dance videos.

3 A sports company asked Daisy to …
  A wear their sports clothes in her videos.
  B do a live dance performance in one of their shops.
  C take photos of their clothes for her next video.

4 Daisy loves …
  A knowing who her followers are.
  B looking at things in different ways and being creative.
  C reading about her followers.

5 Influencers have to …
  A be interesting people.
  B work in fashion.
  C find new things to post about regularly.

6 Daisy needs to …
  A use different types of technology when she's making a video.
  B buy a new phone soon.
  C find a different way to make videos.

DIALOGUE

1 **Complete the dialogues with the phrases in the list.**

had better get | have to help me | made me
make me do it | need to finish | should leave

1 **Maria** Hi, Lara. How did your audition go yesterday?
  Lara I don't think I'll get a part in the school play.
  Maria How come?
  Lara I made a mess of the audition. I couldn't remember my lines. It was awful. Then they _____ sing. And that was worse. You know I can't sing in tune.

2 **Jake** You _____ with the washing up, Sarah. Mum told you to.
  Sarah I can't. I'm busy. I _____ this essay.
  Jake You're always busy. You never do anything around the house.
  Sarah Oh, no. Here we go.
  Jake You're always on your phone or on your laptop. I always have to do the washing up. It's not fair.
  Sarah You can't _____ , Jake.
  Jake No, I can't, but Mum can and she's just come home now.

3 **Toni** What's the matter with you?
  Joe I'm just tired. That's all.
  Toni Why are you so tired?
  Joe I'm not sure. Mind you, I did go to sleep really late last night. I started browsing the internet and I couldn't stop.
  Toni That explains it then. You _____ some sleep now. And you _____ your phone in the living room at night. If it's not in your bedroom, you won't be able to go online. Problem solved.

2 **Now write a dialogue (6–8 lines). Complain to a friend that he/she is spending too much time in front of a screen. Give your friend some advice. Include some of the words in the list.**

had better | have to / don't have to
let | make | must / mustn't | need to
should / shouldn't

B2 First for Schools

1   **You are going to read about five people's experiences of online learning. For questions 1–10, choose from the texts (A–E). The texts may be chosen more than once. In which text does the writer mention:**

   1   losing motivation because of a lack of feedback?

   2   their enjoyment at communicating with other course members?

   3   being surprised by how much variety online learning gave?

   4   technological problems having an impact on learning?

   5   the speed at which teachers responded to her questions?

   6   getting used to the new way of learning relatively quickly?

   7   feeling satisfaction with being able to study flexibly?

   8   learning more than with traditional face-to-face lessons?

   9   finding the assignments extremely challenging?

   10   their ability to concentrate while studying at home?

EXAM GUIDE:

In this part of the exam you have to read a long text split into several sections, or four to six shorter texts about the same topic.

Part 7 tests your ability to locate specific information and recognise and understand opinion and attitude.

There are 10 questions in Part 7 of the Reading and Use of English exam. You must match a question to the correct text or section of text.

Read each text carefully to get an overall understanding before you answer the questions.

Read the questions, skimming and scanning each text or section quickly to find the information which matches each question.

A: I've recently finished doing an online IT course. I must admit that my expectations weren't that high, but I'm convinced that I wouldn't have ended up with as many new skills as I have if I'd gone to classes at college. I had the occasional problem with internet connection during tutorials, but I soon sorted them out. One thing that caught me by surprise was that whenever I posted a query about something, I got a response within minutes. I was expecting to wait for several hours at best. I contributed quite a bit to the chatroom to begin with at least. It soon got a bit like social media rather than a serious means of discussing things.

B: I was unsure whether to do my master's degree in art history online or at university, but eventually opted for the former. The course itself was excellent: well-structured and engaging, with a nice range of topics and activities. There were too many distractions at certain times, with children running around the house and so on, so had to plan my study times carefully. It was delightful to be able to discuss art history-related issues with so many like-minded students in the course chatroom. I really wasn't looking forward to doing the essays and other coursework. The outstanding support we got from the tutors, however, meant that they were nowhere near as demanding as I was expecting.

C: It took me about two years to complete a creative writing course. I would have preferred to do it face-to-face rather than online, but just didn't have time or energy to go to college after a day at work. There was something strangely rewarding about logging on and studying for a couple of hours after everyone else was in bed.

One of my initial doubts about online courses was that I expected we would be given very similar things to do over and over again, so it might get a bit boring, but the opposite was actually the case. This really helped all of the participants to keep our enthusiasm as high as possible throughout the course.

D: I never thought I'd end up doing a psychology course online, but it was an interesting experience. I'm not that computer-literate, so if anything had gone wrong with that side of things, I wouldn't have known what to do. Luckily, that was never an issue and I surprised myself by being able to find my way around the virtual learning environment within just a few days. The materials and coursework were reasonably similar to what you'd get on more traditional courses. We were given a mark for everything we handed in, but the teachers rarely gave us suggestions on how it could be improved, which had a definite effect on my level of interest in the course as a whole.

E: The teachers on the online microbiology course I did couldn't have done more to explain what I'd done well and not so well in the coursework we had to complete. I'm so glad about this, actually, as a lot of what I'd written wasn't really what they were looking for. I've never studied the subject at this level before, so I guess it's not surprising. Part of the problem was that the online system they use for presenting lessons and information didn't work on my laptop for the first few weeks and I never really caught up. Despite all that, I got a lot from it, but think I might go back to in-class lessons with a teacher for any future courses I do.

6 BETTER TOGETHER

→ SB p.58

GRAMMAR
Comparatives

1 ★☆☆ **Look at the website and mark the sentences T (true) or F (false).**

✈ WWW.TRAVELCOMPARE.COM

| Home | News | Advice | Travel finder | Reviews | Q |

London – Paris

	Journey time	Price	Comfort	Frequency	Number of passengers per week	OVERALL experience
Euroair	50 mins	£350	★★★★★	Mon, Tues and Fri	200	★★★★★
Budgetline	1h 15 mins	£21	★	Wed, Fri and Sat	200	★

1 Euroair is not nearly as quick as Budgetline. ☐
2 Budgetline is far more frequent than Euroair. ☐
3 Budgetline is not nearly as good as Euroair. ☐
4 Budgetline is much cheaper than Euroair. ☐
5 Euroair is much more unpopular than Budgetline. ☐
6 Budgetline is a lot slower than Euroair. ☐
7 Euroair is much better than Budgetline. ☐
8 Budgetline is nowhere near as expensive as Euroair. ☐

2 ★★★ **Look at the website again and use the words in brackets to make sentences about the London to Paris flights.**

0 (nowhere near / comfortable)
   Budgetline is nowhere near as comfortable as Euroair.

1 (much / expensive)
   _____

2 (just as / popular)
   _____

3 (far / quick)
   _____

4 (nowhere near / good)
   _____

5 (just as / frequent)
   _____

6 (not nearly / cheap)
   _____

3 ★★☆ **Rewrite the sentences using the adjective in brackets and an expression with ... and ... .**

0 The boys just won't stop growing. (tall)
   The boys are growing taller and taller.

1 Every year there are more cars on the road. (busy)
   _____

2 I love spring. Every day the sun stays up a few minutes later. (long)
   _____

3 Scientists say the temperature of the Earth is increasing. (hot)
   _____

4 The price of food is increasing by the week. (expensive)
   _____

4 ★★★ **Rewrite the sentences using a comparative expression with *the ..., the ... .***

0 Loud music gives me a bad headache.
   The louder the music gets the worse my headache gets.

1 Hot weather makes me angry.
   _____

2 Driving fast is dangerous.
   _____

3 When you're hungry, food tastes better.
   _____

4 Old people need less sleep.
   _____

Linkers of contrast → SB p.61

5 ⭐☆☆ **Match the parts of the sentences.**

1 Although not many people came to the party, ☐
2 I feel really tired today ☐
3 Liam invited Dan to his party ☐
4 In spite of having sold millions of books, ☐
5 The film was in French, so I didn't understand much. ☐
6 The athlete wasn't 100 percent fit. ☐

a even though they're not the best of friends.
b no one knows who the author is.
c However, I still really enjoyed it.
d Nevertheless, she still won the race easily.
e we still had a great time.
f despite having had a really good night's sleep.

6 ⭐⭐☆ **Complete the card with the missing linkers.**

¹A_ _ _ou_ _ you annoy me at least once a day.
²I_ _ _i_e o_ the fact you always get your way.
³E_e_ _ _ou_ _ you take things without saying 'please'.
And ⁴_e_ _i_e the mess in my room that you leave.
It seems I don't like you. ⁵_e_e_ _ _e_e_ _,
that's not true.
There's something I need to say about you.
It seems we're so different. ⁶_o_e_e_,
we're not.
You are my sister – the best friend that I've got.

7 ⭐⭐⭐ **Combine the two sentences using the word in brackets.**

Unusual facts about me

0 I'm short. I'm good at basketball. (despite)
  Despite being short, I'm good at basketball.

1 I've got two bikes. I can't ride a bike. (although)
  _____

2 My mum's French. I don't speak French. (however)
  _____

3 I love Italian food. I don't like pizza. (even though)
  _____

4 I always go to bed early. I'm always late for school. (nevertheless)
  _____

5 I'm 175 cm tall. I'm only 14. (in spite of)
  _____

GET IT RIGHT!

however

Learners often use *however* incorrectly.

✓ *I looked back in his direction. However, he had vanished.*

✗ *I looked back in his direction however, he had vanished.*

Match the sentences and rewrite them using *however*.

0 Tom asked Elena out.
  Tom asked Elena out. However, she said no.

1 Ethan was offered the position of school counsellor.
  _____

2 Loom bands used to be a big craze.
  _____

3 The passengers were stuck on the train for two hours.
  _____

4 My friends did a 10K run for charity last month.
  _____

5 Hundreds of people volunteered to help the doctors and nurses.
  _____

a ~~She said no.~~
b Nobody spoke to each other.
c He turned it down.
d A lot of them didn't have any training.
e I hurt my knee and couldn't do it with them.
f It seems to be over now.

VOCABULARY
Ways of speaking → SB p.58

1 ★☆☆ **Unscramble the verbs and then match them to the correct nouns.**

verb

1 arispe _____ ☐
2 stugesg _____ ☐
3 feedin _____ ☐
4 irecitsic _____ ☐
5 tamid _____ ☐
6 toridnceu _____ ☐

noun

a suggestion
b criticism
c admission
d introduction
e praise
f definition

2 ★★☆ **Circle the correct options.**

1 'You've all done really well in the test. I'm so proud of you.'
   Giving *criticism / a definition / praise.*
2 'That colour doesn't suit you.'
   Making a/an *introduction / criticism / suggestion*
3 'Why don't we go to the new pizza place?'
   Making a/an *suggestion / admission / praise*
4 'I dropped your phone and broke it. Sorry.'
   Making a/an *definition / criticism / admission*
5 'Harry, I'd like you to meet Tom.'
   Making a/an *introduction / praise / criticism*
6 'A friend is a person you know well and who you like a lot.'
   Giving a/an *criticism / definition / admission*

3 ★★☆ **Complete the sentences with the missing verbs.**

1 'OK, it was me. I ate the last piece of cake,' she _____ .
2 'You _____ the word 'creative' really clearly. Thank you.'
3 'The coach _____ the team even though they lost the match.'
4 'Why don't you read this book? I think you'll enjoy it. it's great,' he _____ .
5 He _____ me to Sam. 'Sam, this is Dan. Dan, this is Sam.'
6 'Dan _____ everyone the last time we worked with him. It wasn't very nice.'

Friendship idioms → SB p.59

4 ★★☆ **Choose the correct response (A or B).**

1 If you're feeling sad or upset any time, I'm here for you.
   A You can bury the hatchet. ☐
   B You can have my shoulder to cry on. ☐
2 Izzy and Amalia like each other a lot and they've become friends really quickly.
   A They get on like a house on fire. ☐
   B They fall out all the time. ☐
3 We decided to stop arguing and become friends again.
   A So we fell out. ☐
   B So we buried the hatchet. ☐
4 Annie and her twin look exactly the same.
   A They're like two peas in a pod. ☐
   B They get on like a house on fire. ☐
5 Max hasn't spoken to Piotr since Piotr broke his games console.
   A They're joined at the hip. ☐
   B They fell out when Piotr broke his games console. ☐
6 Sadie and Isa are always together.
   A I think they cleared the air. ☐
   B I think they're joined at the hip. ☐
7 My best friend always knows how I'm feeling, even if I haven't told her.
   A She knows me inside out. ☐
   B She usually buries the hatchet. ☐
8 I had a big argument with my parents, but there are no bad feelings between us now.
   A The argument has cleared the air. ☐
   B The argument has fallen out. ☐

5 ★★☆ **Complete the idioms.**

1 Olivia and Clara had an argument last week, but they're friends again now. They decided to bury the _____ .
2 Toni isn't talking to me after I posted that photo of him last week. We need to clear _____ .
3 Abby and Freya are joined _____ – they're really close and they're always together.
4 My best friend has known me since we were three. She knows me _____ .
5 Did you _____ out with Ana? I haven't seen you together in a while.
6 When you're feeling sad, I'm here. You can have a _____ to cry on any time.
7 Lila and Nora aren't twins, but they look like two _____ .
8 Alex and Lewis have only known each other for a few weeks, but they get on like a _____ .

REFERENCE

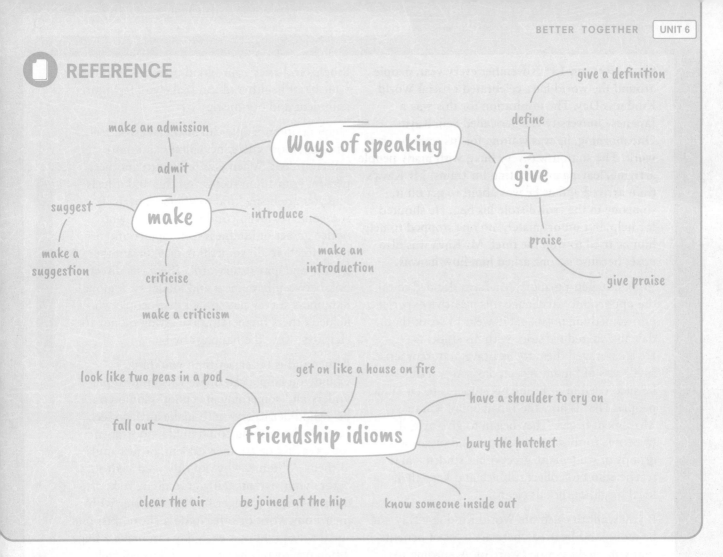

VOCABULARY EXTRA

1 **Complete the sentences with the words in the list.**

> affectionate | forgiving
> kind-hearted | loyal
> supportive | thoughtful

A friend who ...

1 always likes and supports you even when other people don't, is _____ .

2 helps and encourages you when things are difficult is _____ .

3 likes other people a lot and is always happy to help them is _____ .

4 shows you they like you is _____ .

5 lets you make mistakes and understands and accepts your weaknesses is _____ .

2 **Complete the posts with adjectives from Exercise 1.**

| Home | About | Top news | 🔍 |

My person of the week is … 👍 💬 🔁

It's my best friend, Aimi. She's very patient with me and is always there for me. I can cry on her shoulder any time of the day or night. She's listened to me a lot recently and helped me make some BIG decisions. She's so ¹_____ . She's a ²_____ friend because when I do or say something wrong, she never minds even if other people don't agree with me. When I make a mistake or forget something, she's ³_____ . Aimi deserves to be person of the week every week! **Lina**

It's my little brother. He's only four. He brings me presents from nursery and draws pictures for me. His favourite thing is to sit close to me and our cat on the sofa and watch his favourite cartoon with us. He's ⁴_____ and ⁵_____ with everyone, including the cat! **Lewis**

3 **Choose your own 'person of the week' and write a post like the ones in Exercise 2.**

_____

_____

_____

Since 1997, on 13ᵗʰ November every year, people around the world have celebrated official World Kindness Day. The inspiration for this was a Japanese university teacher called Seiji Kaya. One morning, he was waiting for his train to go to work. The station was very busy, with many people arriving, leaving and waiting for trains. Mr Kaya's train arrived and as he was about to get on it, someone in the crowd stole his bag. He shouted for help, but unfortunately, no one stopped to help him or tried to stop the thief. Mr Kaya was also upset because no one asked him how he was.

Instead of getting angry, Mr Kaya decided to take the opportunity to change this negative experience into something positive. He went to work that day and shared his story with his students. He encouraged them to 'be brave and to practise small acts of kindness each day'. As a result, he succeeded in inspiring his students to be kinder people. That is how the Japan Small Kindness Movement began. They began to give awards to people for doing kind things and organised groups of students to greet other students and teachers and to collect rubbish and keep their local neighbourhoods clean.

If you want to celebrate World Kindness Day and be more kind-hearted, there are a lot of benefits that you might not be aware of. According to researchers, helping someone can also help you, without you even realising. When you are kind, your body produces a chemical called oxytocin which is sometimes called the 'love' hormone.

It helps to lower your blood pressure, improve your heart health and can make you feel more confident and optimistic.

Helping other people can also make you feel stronger, more energetic, calmer and more self-confident. When you're kind to another person, your brain recognises this and it feels like you are being kind to yourself, or as if someone has given you praise. People who notice an act of kindness feel happier and are more likely to do something nice for another person and 'pay it forward'. There is a direct link between happiness and kindness. A global happiness survey has shown that people who helped others financially, like giving money to charities, were the happiest by far.

Being kind is far easier than you think. Could you help a classmate when they don't understand something at school? Could you be a shoulder to cry on to make a friend feel better? Perhaps you could hold a door open for a teacher or another student, or just smile at them. At home, why not tidy your bedroom before your parents tell you to do it? Ask, or offer to help a younger brother or sister with their homework or offer to do a chore. Just one small act of kindness each day can make a huge difference to another person and to yourself. So why not volunteer in your community, raise money for a charity and make kindness part of your everyday routine? #WorldKindnessDay #BeKindEveryDay

READING

1 **Read the text quickly. Choose the best title.**

A The most important day ☐
B Be kind to others and yourself ☐
C The worst feeling ever ☐

2 **Read the article again and answer the questions.**

1 When did World Kindness Day start?

2 When do people celebrate World Kindness Day?

3 Which country did it start in?

4 Why did Mr Kaya start World Kindness Day?

5 What is oxytocin and how can it help our health?

6 What is the connection between kindness and happiness?

3 CRITICAL THINKING **Read the situation and the responses. Which response do you think is the kindest? Why? How would you respond?**

A student in your class doesn't have a laptop. A special school project is due next week and it must be presented using a laptop.

1 Offer to lend them their laptop for the weekend.
2 Offer to give them an old laptop to keep.
3 Offer to help them talk to the teacher and ask to present the project in a different way.

4 **Think about an act of kindness that you did for someone or that someone did for you. Write a short paragraph describing it (80–100 words). Think about how you felt and how it made the other person feel.**

DEVELOPING *Writing*

An essay

1 INPUT **Read Lola's essay. Which charity does she want to support?**

1   I want our school to support Water Aid this year. It provides access to clean water for some of the poorest people in the world, or places for them to go and get water. For example, 785 million people around the world do not have access to water close to their home. That is one in 10 people. Three billion people cannot wash their hands at home.

2   Not having access to clean water also affects children's health and education. Around the world, more than 700,000 children die every year because they drink dirty water and get ill. More than 443 million school days are lost every year because of water-related illnesses. Every day, 2,000 children die because they don't have clean water and providing clean water could decrease the number of childhood deaths by at least one third.

3   WaterAid is a good example of how access to clean water also gives communities important skills for life. People can learn how to repair taps and about the importance of good hygiene. These skills can help to break the cycle of poverty and disease.

4   In my opinion, water is a basic human right and we should all have access to it. I think that we should support this charity because our donations can change the lives of thousands of people for the better.

2   Read the essay again and answer the questions.

1   How many people do not have access to clean water?

_____

2   How many children die every day because of water-related diseases?

_____

3   What other skills do people learn when they have access to clean water?

_____

3 ANALYSE **Put the information in the order the writer mentions it.**

☐ a   the problems people face without clean water
☐ b   other skills people learn / benefits of clean water
☐ c   the writer's opinion
☐ d   the charity and what it does

4 PLAN **Imagine that you want your school to start supporting a charity. You can choose the charity below or a charity that is important to you. Make notes for each paragraph.**

African Wildlife Foundation:

based in Nairobi, Kenya; protects Africa's most endangered species through wildlife conservation, land and habitat protection; helps local people and wildlife to learn to live together

5 PRODUCE **Write your essay (200–250 words). Use your notes in Exercise 4. Make sure you include all the points in the checklist.**

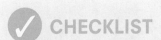

✓ **CHECKLIST**

☐   Make sure you explain which charity you want to support and what it does.
☐   Include examples of facts and statistics and other benefits of the charity.
☐   Try and show a good range of vocabulary.
☐   Make your opinion clear in the last paragraph.

🎧 LISTENING

1 🔊 6.01 **Listen and match the pictures with the dialogues.**

A ☐

B ☐

C ☐

2 🔊 6.01 **Listen again and answer the questions.**

1 1 Which is more expensive: the music festival or the train trip?

_____

2 What do they decide to do?

_____

2 3 Where is Bradley from?

_____

4 Why does Matteo want Diana to introduce him to Bradley?

_____

3 5 Why is Molly upset?

_____

6 What did Martha do?

_____

3 🔊 6.01 **Complete the sentences. Listen again and check.**

1 **Tom** I'd rather not fly to be honest. It's m_____ b_____ for the environment.

Olly Good point. What about the coast to coast cycle ride? It's n_____ n_____ as expensive as the music festival or the train trip.

2 **Diana** He's also m_____ t_____ than I thought.

Diana Basketball is j_____ as p_____ in Texas as it is here.

3 **Emma** That's e_____ the best way to sort it out.

Molly The l_____ it goes on, the w_____ I feel.

DIALOGUE

1 **Put the sentences in order to make a dialogue.**

☐ **Dad** It's a ten-minute walk!

☐ **Dad** You know what? I've got a good idea. You drive the kids in the car or taxi or whatever. I'll take the train and we'll all meet on the beach.

☐ **Dad** No chance, I thought we'd make it a tech free day, too. Just a good old family day out on the train.

☐ **Dad** I thought we'd go to Prestatyn. It's by far a nicer beach.

☐ **Dad** Who fancies a day at the beach?

☐ **Dad** I said how about a beach day, not a shopping day. Tim, how about you?

☐ **Dad** I'm not. It's a whole lot easier than taking the car. And the train's quicker, too. It's easily the best option.

☐ **Mum** We'll probably miss the train and have to wait hours for the next one.

☐ **Mum** That sounds like a great idea. Shall we go to Llandudno?

☐ **Mum** Well, I'm not so sure. I think I agree with the kids on this one. It's miles more convenient to take the car. I mean we've got to get to the station …

☐ **Lucy** But Llandudno's got better shops by far.

☐ **Lucy** The train?! Please tell me you're joking.

☐ **Tim** Yeah, Dad. Please tell us you're joking.

☐ **Tim** Can I take my tablet with me?

☐ **Tim** It'd be even quicker if we took a taxi.

2 **Imagine the family are on the beach. They are deciding where to eat lunch. Write a dialogue (8–10 lines). Use some comparative structures.**

> **PRONUNCIATION**
> Linking words with /dʒ/ and /tʃ/ Go to page 119. 🎧

You are going to read a magazine article about a mobile art exhibition. Six sentences have been removed from the article. Choose from the sentences A–G the one which best fits each gap (1–6). There is one extra sentence which you do not need to use.

Art on the Move

MuMo is the name of the world's first mobile museum of contemporary art. It was first set up in 2011 as part of an initiative which aimed to make contemporary art more accessible to school students and other young people.

When you see MuMo arriving in your town or village, you immediately recognise why it is called 'mobile'. The museum building is actually made up of a large freight container that travels from place to place on the back of a large articulated truck. 1_____ But apart from the name, which is written in extremely large letters on the side, you'd have no idea that they were in there.

Once installed at its destination, whether it's a town square, a car park or a school playground, the container is transformed into an art exhibition. 2_____ Each of these is devoted to a particular art form, so you can see not only painting, but also sculpture and installation art as well as video and design. Young people are invited in to come and walk around and admire the works of art on display.

Mumo was the brainchild of a French businesswoman called Ingrid Brochard, who came up with the idea in 2011. Since then, it has travelled around various European countries and has even been on a trip to Africa. Because it takes the form of a container, the mobile museum is even more mobile than it might at first appear. 3_____ This explains how it has managed to reach places so far away from its base in France.

The idea behind the project was to bring contemporary art to young people in more remote regions, who perhaps wouldn't otherwise get the chance to see it. 4_____ In its first five years it was visited by as many as 150,000 people in the target age group, half of whom had never been to art museum before. In each of its destinations, the museum is open daily from 8.30 am to 7 pm and there is no entrance charge. During the week, no adult visitors are allowed in the museum, although this rule is relaxed at weekends.

Once inside the museum, visitors soon become immersed in different worlds and can freely explore the art. As Ingrid Brochard points out, at school we're taught to read and write, but it's also important to learn how to dream, to imagine and to connect to our emotions. 5_____ Although some teenagers may feel nervous about coming along at first, once a few friends have tried, the word soon gets round. That's because it's a fun experience.

What's more, recent additions to the original idea of the mobile museum include hands-on workshops that complement the tours. 6_____ They see, for example, how some of the effects they have seen in the exhibition can be achieved, and they get the chance to have a go themselves.

In one recent project, MuMo teamed up with the Centre Pompidou in Paris to take works of art from one of France's most prestigious museums way beyond its four walls. Modern masterpieces by such artists as Chagall, Picasso and Mondrian were amongst those that hit the road, and these featured alongside a full programme of creative workshops and events.

A That's what art can do for young people.

B This was its most ambitious trip so far.

C These help young visitors to become more familiar with the creative possibilities of art.

D It's certainly fulfilled that aim.

E This is displayed over two floors and is divided into four distinct zones.

F For example, it can easily travel by boat before being loaded onto a truck.

G Carefully packed away inside are twenty pieces of contemporary art.

CONSOLIDATION

🎧 LISTENING

1 🔊 6.03 **Listen to Sam talking about how he met his best friend Viktor and answer the questions.**

1 What instrument did Viktor play in the band?
_____

2 How many members were there in the band?
_____

3 Where did Sam work?
_____

4 How did Viktor respond when Sam told him he knew him from the band?
_____

2 🔊 6.03 **Listen again and mark the sentences T (true) or F (false).**

1 Viktor's band had some local support. ☐

2 Viktor always played his trumpet at the front of the stage. ☐

3 Sam tried to talk to Viktor when he was in a band. ☐

4 Sam was Viktor's boss at the theatre. ☐

5 Sam kept his secret from Viktor forever. ☐

6 Viktor was embarrassed when he found out Sam knew he used to be in a band. ☐

🄖 GRAMMAR

3 **Match the parts of the sentences.**

1 You had better leave soon ☐
2 You're supposed to arrive before 9 am ☐
3 The test was really difficult ☐
4 There was a lot of traffic ☐
5 The more I listen to the new Lewis Capaldi album, ☐
6 Dad says it's getting more ☐
7 Even though I didn't know anyone there, ☐
8 In spite of really studying hard, ☐

a but somehow I managed to pass.
b and we were only just able to get to the airport in time.
c and more difficult to find parking in the city centre.
d I failed the test badly.
e if you don't want to get a 'late' mark.
f I still really enjoyed the party.
g if you don't want to miss the train.
h the more I like it.

🄰z VOCABULARY

4 **Complete the missing words.**

1 To c_____ to the internet you need a w_____ r_____ .

2 To p_____ your laptop in you need a p_____ l_____ and an a_____ if you're in a foreign country.

3 If you want to do video conferencing you need a w_____ and maybe a h_____ .

4 To keep your phone safe you should use a p_____ c_____ .

5 To connect your keyboard to your computer you might use a U_____ p_____ .

6 If your laptop is out of power you will need to use the c_____ .

7 If your computer is slow when you b_____ the internet, you need to u_____ your system.

8 This software lets you s_____ your laptop and your phone so they're always up-to-date with each other.

5 **Use one word from each list to complete the statements. There are two extra words in each list.**

> admit | criticise | define
> introduce | praise | suggest

> a protective case | bury the hatchet | clear the air
> fall out | headset | a house on fire

1 'Will you _____ me to the new boy today?'
Yes, of course. I'm sure you'll get on with each other like _____ .

2 'I'm really sorry. I _____ I made a mistake and I was wrong.'
That's OK. Why don't we _____ and forget about it?

3 'What would you _____ as a present for Kim's birthday?'
'She's always dropping her phone. What about _____ ?'

4 'Please don't _____ the other people in the group. We need to work as a team.'
'Sorry. I don't want to _____ about this.'

DIALOGUE

6 **Put the sentences in order to make a dialogue.**

Olivia No, I'm tired of doing that. They never fix it properly. It's time for a new one.

Olivia What? Today is Monday. I'm not waiting five days. I'm off to the shops. Now!

Olivia Not if they don't fix it properly. It will just be a waste of my time.

Olivia You always say that, but then you never do.

Olivia I don't know. I was trying to save a document and the whole computer crashed.

Olivia I don't believe it. My laptop's broken again.

Liam It sounds serious. You'd better take it to the repair shop.

Liam Well I will this time. I promise. I'll take a look at it over the weekend.

Liam Again? What is it this time?

Liam What! It will be miles cheaper to get it fixed. It's the best solution by far.

Liam Well at least let me have a look at it first. Maybe I can fix it.

READING

7 **Read the article and put the events in order.**

☐ 1 He connects the hose pipe with the toilet.

☐ 2 The boy is presented with a bill to pay.

☐ 3 He asks the club for help.

☐ 4 The boy is fishing on a lake with his friends.

☐ 5 He loses his phone.

☐ 6 The police question the boy about his actions.

☐ 7 The club owner arrives.

☐ 8 Water pours into the club.

☐ 9 He arrives at the club with equipment to help him find his phone.

Desperate measures

The amount of time that teenagers spend in front of a screen is a huge concern for many parents all over the world. But are they worrying unnecessarily? After all, didn't their parents worry about how much time they spent in front of the TV every day? Aren't computers just the modern-day equivalent of the television or is it more than that? Many experts seem to think that many teenagers are actually addicted to technology and would find it very difficult to spend a day without it.

The parents of one 16-year-old boy in Germany may have agreed with them when they found out just how far their son would go for his mobile phone. The boy was on a fishing trip in a boat on a small lake with his friends when his phone slipped out of his hand and fell into the water – gone forever, so it would seem. But the boy refused to accept that that would be the last he would ever see of it. Even though he knew that the phone itself would be ruined, he was determined to retrieve the data card it contained with all his contact information and photos on it. This information was far too important to lose, so he started to think about what he could do to find the phone.

His first plan involved asking the fishing club that owned the lake if he could borrow a diving suit and jump into the water to search for the phone. Unsurprisingly, they decided he couldn't and advised him to give up trying to find it. It was then he realised this was something he was going to have to do on his own when no one was watching. So later that night, he went back to the lake with two water pumps and some hose pipes. His idea was simple. He was going to drain all the water out of the lake and find his phone lying at the bottom.

He decided that the best place to pump the water into would be the club's toilet. He managed to connect one end of the pipe to the pump and put the other end into the toilet. However, what he didn't know was that the toilet was connected to a small tank rather than a larger sewer system. The result was that the tank was quickly filled up and the water started to flood into the club car park. The boy tried to stop the flow, but the more he tried, the worse the situation got and before he knew it, there was water everywhere. When the club owner arrived, he immediately called the police, leaving the boy with a lot of explaining to do. Sadly, the boy was unable to find his phone. All he got was a big bill for the cost of cleaning up the mess he had created.

WRITING

8 **Write a paragraph of about 120 words about an occasion when you had a problem with technology.**

- Explain what the problem was.
- Write about how it affected you.
- Say what you did to try and solve the problem.

7 ROSE-TINTED GLASSES

Grammar video
▶18

ⓖ GRAMMAR
Ways of referring to the future (review)
→ SB p.68

1 ★☆☆ **Write sentences with the correct future form of the verbs.**

0 I / play / tennis / with Milly / tomorrow
   I'm playing tennis with Milly tomorrow.

1 My dad / go / to / Berlin / on business / next month
   _____

2 The / lesson / start / in / ten minutes
   _____

3 As soon as / Mum / get / home / we / go / to / the cinema
   _____

4 We / not have dinner / until / Dad / come / home
   _____

5 Tina and Tom / stay / with / their aunt / in / Mexico / in / the summer holidays
   _____

2 ★★☆ **Complete the dialogue with the correct form of the verbs. Use the present continuous or *going to*.**

Phoebe ⁰ _____*Are you coming*_____ (you / come) on the school trip this summer?

Nathan I'm not sure. I ¹_____ (ask) my parents this evening.

Phoebe Matt and Lucy ²_____ (not plan) to come. They ³_____ (travel) overland to Turkey with their family this summer.

Nathan That sounds exciting.

Phoebe Yes, they ⁴_____ (drive) across France, Switzerland and Italy. Then they ⁵_____ (take) a car ferry from Italy to Turkey, via Greece.

Nathan Awesome! When ⁶_____ (Mr Jones / hold) the meeting about the school trip?

Phoebe He ⁷_____ (organise) it for next Saturday at 2 pm.

3 ★★☆ **Complete the dialogues with the correct future form of the verbs in brackets.**

1 **A** What _____ (you / do) on Saturday evening?
   B I _____ (go) to a concert with my sister.

2 **A** Do you think your mum _____ (let) you come and stay for the weekend?
   B Yes, I think so. I _____ (ask) her tonight.

3 **A** What time _____ (the football match / start) on Saturday?
   B It _____ (start) at two o'clock.

4 **A** I _____ (look for) a Saturday job. I'd like to work in a clothes shop.
   B Really? My brother and I _____ (join) a climbing club, so I can't get a Saturday job.

5 **A** It's my birthday tomorrow. I hope it _____ (be) sunny because we _____ (have) a barbecue in the afternoon!
   B I don't think it _____ (rain) tomorrow. The weather's been so nice today.

6 **A** What time _____ (the train / leave)?
   B It _____ (leave) at six o'clock.

4 ★★☆ **Will it happen or won't it happen? Read the notes and write sentences.**

0 Scientists (build) a lift into space.
   Scientists won't build a lift into space.

1 Your computer (have) a sense of smell.
   _____

2 Facebook still (be) the most popular social network.
   _____

3 Robots (do) all the work on farms.
   _____

4 People (go) on holiday in space.
   _____

5 We (be able to) upload the contents of our brains to our computers.
   _____

6 People (be able to) touch each other through their phones.
   _____

Future continuous and future perfect

→ SB p.69

5 ★☆☆ **Write sentences using the future continuous.**

The holiday's finally here. I'm so excited.
This time tomorrow …

1 I / swim / in the sea

_____

2 Sam / sit / on the beach / with his phone

_____

3 Mum / explore / the town

_____

4 Dad / buy / food / at the local market

_____

6 ★★☆ **Complete the dialogues using the future perfect.**

1 A We're late. They _____
everything by the time we get there. (eat)

B I'm sure they _____
something for us. (leave)

2 A Hi, Miriam. I thought you were coming
round to my house this afternoon.
Everyone's here.

B I am coming. I'll be there at six.

A But everybody _____
home by then. (go)

3 A Are you looking forward to the charity
swimming event tomorrow?

B Yes. By this time tomorrow, we
_____ across the
Bosphorus from Asia to Europe. (swim)

4 A Have you got any plans for the future?

B Yes. By the time I'm thirty, I
_____ around the
world. (travel)

7 ★★☆ **Choose the correct options.**

1 A Dad's plane lands at eight o'clock.

B It's 8.30 now. His plane *will be landing* /
will have landed.

2 A Hey, you're going to the beach this
weekend, right?

B Yes, by this time on Saturday, I *will be
swimming* / *will swim* in the sea.

3 A By the time I'm 18, I *will be leaving* /
will have left school. I'm sure.

B Me too!

4 A The show starts at 7 pm.

B Sorry, I can't come. I *will be eating* / *will eat*
dinner with my family at that time.

5 A Mum, I'm going round to Matt's house now.

B What about your homework?

A I *will have done* / *will do* it later.

8 ★★☆ **Complete the email with the phrases in the list.**

'll be | 'll be going | 'll be having | 'll be staying
'll have been shopping' | 'll have seen | 'll have visited
'll send | 'll text

Antonia
Antonia@thinkmail.com

Hey Lily,

Well, this time tomorrow, I ¹_____ in
London. How cool is that! We ²_____
at a hotel on the South Bank. It's near the Globe Theatre.
I ³_____ you a photo when we get
there. I know you love anything to do with the theatre
and everything about Shakespeare! On the first day, we
⁴_____ to the Tower of London. My mum's
keen to see the Crown Jewels. I just want to see the ravens
and the Beefeaters, of course. Oh, yes! And guess what?
We ⁵_____ lunch in Speedy's Sandwich
Bar and Café on North Gower Street – the one that
Benedict Cumberbatch always goes to in the TV series
Sherlock. I can't wait.

So anyway, by the end of the trip, I ⁶_____
the London Dungeons. I ⁷_____ the view
from the top of the Shard, and I ⁸_____
at Camden Market. Amazing!

I ⁹_____ you as soon as I get there.

See you soon.

Antonia

GET IT RIGHT!

will

Learners often confuse *would* and *will*.

✓ I think it will be a good experience.

✗ I think it would be a good experience.

Complete the sentences with *will* or *would*.

1 I hope the exam _____ be OK, but to be
honest, I'm dreading it.

2 If Dan wasn't such a pessimist, he _____ be
much more fun to be with.

3 We're about to go out, so I _____ call you later.

4 Thanks for the offer. I _____ be very happy
to accept.

5 Sally's really looking forward to visiting us. We
_____ have a great time.

6 My mum is on the point of changing her job. She
_____ like to spend less time commuting.

VOCABULARY
Phrases to talk about the future

1 ⭐☆☆ **Complete the missing words.**

1 A Hi, Helen. I was on the p_____
of calling you.

B Really? That's strange.

2 A I'm o_____ to the cinema. I'll see
you later.

B OK. Enjoy the film.

3 A We're a_____ to have dinner.
Would you like to join us?

B That's OK thanks. I've just eaten.

4 A We're d_____ to go on holiday
next week.

B That's exciting. Where are you going?

2 ⭐⭐☆ **Match the parts of the sentences.
Then match them with the pictures.**

1 I always feel nervous when I'm about ☐
2 We are on the point of ☐
3 I'm off ☐
4 We're due to ☐

a to go to the dentist's.
b to the park. Would you like to come?
c move house tomorrow.
d finishing the experiment.

3 ⭐⭐⭐ **Write true sentences for you using the
phrases in brackets.**

1 (about to) _____
_____

2 (on the point of) _____

3 (due to) _____

4 (off to) _____

Feelings about future events

4 ⭐⭐☆ **Match sentences 1–6 with the sentences
with similar meaning a–f.**

1 I'm feeling quite apprehensive. ☐
2 I'm dreading it. ☐
3 I've got a good feeling about it. ☐
4 I'm a bit unsure about it. ☐
5 I'm getting so worked up about it. ☐
6 I just don't know where to start. ☐

a I think it's going to be fine.
b I'm a bit nervous.
c I'm a little uncertain about it.
d I'm not looking forward to it at all.
e I'm not sure what to do first.
f It's really upsetting me.

WordWise
Expressions with *so*

5 ⭐⭐☆ **Complete the dialogues with
the phrases in the list.**

> I hope so | or so | so far
> so not | so-so | so what?

1 A I'm _____ looking forward to
revising for my exams next month.

B I know. Me neither but let's organise a party
after we've finished them.

2 A How many people will be coming on
Saturday?

B I'm not sure. A hundred people have bought
tickets _____ .

3 A How are you getting on with your guitar
lessons?

B _____ . I'm getting better,
but I need to practise a lot more.

4 A The other team has the best player from
this area in it.

B _____ Our team will still play
well and we'll all do our best.

5 A Will you have finished your essay by
tomorrow?

B _____ . That's the final deadline.
I don't want to miss that.

6 A I've got to tidy my room by lunchtime.

B I've got an hour _____ free.
I'll help you.

REFERENCE

about to

off to

Phrases to talk about the future

due to

on the point of

FEELINGS ABOUT FUTURE EVENTS

Hope for the future

have a really good feeling about something

feel quite positive

be really looking forward to something

Concerns for the future

dread

just not know where to start

be really worried about something

get worked up about

be a bit unsure about

have a bad feeling about something

feel quite apprehensive about something

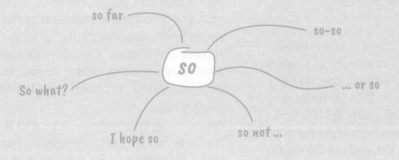

so far

so-so

so

So what?

... or so

I hope so

so not ...

VOCABULARY EXTRA

1   **Complete the definitions with the expressions in the list.**

> a taste of things to come
> any minute now | get round to
> in due course | just around the corner

1   at an appropriate time in the future and not before _____

2   do something that you have intended to do for a long time _____

3   going to happen soon, in the near future _____

4   a brief experience that is the first of similar things that will happen in the future _____

5   very soon _____

2   **Complete the sentences with expressions from Exercise 1.**

1   Students will receive the results of their assessments _____ .

2   I didn't _____ messaging Evie yesterday. I'll do it now.

3   Our exams are _____ . In fact, they start tomorrow!

4   My parents will be home _____ . Quick! Let's tidy up.

5   Helping my dad in his office this summer will be _____ in the world of work.

3   **Complete the sentences so that they are true for you.**

1   Any minute now, I _____

2   My _____ is/are just around the corner.

3   I never get round to _____

4   My parents think they will _____ in due course.

5   _____ was a taste of things to come for me.

What makes you happy?

Have you ever wondered what really makes people happy? Is it chocolate, money, kind and caring family and friends, or a combination of these things?

A _____ ☐

According to research, including the World Happiness Report, money is not the most important factor in our happiness. We all need enough money for things we need, like food or accommodation, but happiness depends more on recognising the people and things you have in your life and appreciating them. For example, upgrading your phone, owning the latest version of something or buying new clothes might make you feel happy at that moment, but the pleasure and enjoyment of that moment does not last, so this is not real happiness.

B _____ ☐

People need to socialise and it is our friendships that make us happy. When we build friendships with other people, it is those relationships that can help us get through bad times. Performing acts of kindness and being generous with your time and talents will also make you and other people feel happier.

C _____ ☐

Simple things like smiling can make you and other people feel good. According to research, 14 percent of people smile fewer than five times a day. More than 30 percent of us smile more than 20 times a day, but young children smile as many as 400 times a day. So why not try smiling more? You'll be surprised how many people smile back. Smiling will stimulate your brain in the same way as eating 2,000 bars of chocolate will – but it's obviously better for your health and your teeth and smiling is a lot cheaper!

D _____ ☐

Take time out to do some exercise and you will be doing your body more good than you think. Poor health or being lazy will not make you happy and it won't make you feel good about yourself. We are designed to move around, so doing exercise even for a short time each day will help to reduce stress and anxiety. It will also release happy chemicals in your brain called endorphins, which will definitely make you feel more positive and optimistic. Go on, get moving!

E _____ ☐

Do you sometimes wake up in the morning and feel tired and moody? It's probably because you haven't had enough sleep. Teenagers in particular often go to bed too late, but have to get up early to go to school. It's highly likely they will not be getting enough sleep. A lack of sleep will affect your mood and your happiness. It will also affect your ability to concentrate and increase your stress levels. So, what's the answer? Try and get at least eight hours of sleep each night and you will notice an improvement in your school work and your mood. Your brain and your body will thank you.

We can't be happy alone, we can't be happy all the time, but we can definitely be happier than we are at the moment. So, what will you be doing to improve your happiness levels?

READING

1 **Read the article and match the headings with the paragraphs. There are two extra headings you do not need.**

   1 Smiling ☐
   2 Sleep ☐
   3 Money ☐
   4 Diet and food ☐
   5 Health and exercise ☐
   6 Music ☐
   7 Relationships ☐

2 **Read the article again and answer the questions.**

   1 According to recent research, what is more important than money to be happy?
   _____
   2 What kind of happiness do we feel from material things?
   _____
   3 Why is spending time with other people important for our happiness?
   _____
   4 What can the result of smiling be?
   _____
   5 How can regular exercise help us feel happier?
   _____
   6 What can happen if you don't get enough sleep?
   _____

3 CRITICAL THINKING **Put the topics from the article in the order that makes you happiest (1 = happiest). Then answer the questions.**

   1 How do you feel if you don't get enough sleep? _____
   2 Which parts of the text do you agree / disagree with? Give reasons. _____

4 **Write a paragraph for the text with your top tip for being happy (80–100 words).**

DEVELOPING Writing

An anecdote

1 INPUT **Read the anecdote and choose the best title.**

A I had a really bad feeling … ☐

B I had a really good feeling … ☐

C I was dreading the moment when … ☐

B *I* U ≡ ≡ ≡ ≡

By Sam Kelly

[A] I play in a band with two of my friends. Our dream is that one day we'll be famous and we'll be doing tours all over the world. Our fans will be screaming for us while we play on stage. After last weekend, our dream is on the point of really happening.

[B] I'm the lead singer and I play the guitar, Harvey plays the drums, and Stella is the bass guitarist. We write all our own songs and we think we're great. We usually play in my garage and we practise three nights a week and at the weekend.

[C] Harvey is always worried about things and he gets really worked up about making mistakes. He wants everything to be perfect. So, when we managed to get our first live gig – an 18th birthday party in the local community centre – he had a bad feeling about it. When we arrived at the party, Harvey was about to go home, but luckily Stella always feels quite positive and she persuaded him to stay and play. You can't have a band without a drummer! I had a really good feeling about it and I felt really excited.

[D] The gig went really well and at the end a music promoter approached us. So, next week we'll be going to a recording studio to play our songs for him. Maybe by this time next year, we'll have recorded our first album. I hope so. Watch this space!

---

2 **Read the anecdote again and answer the questions.**

1 How many band members are there in Main Event?

_____

2 Where does the band practise and how often?

_____

3 What is Harvey like?

_____

4 How did Stella help Harvey?

_____

5 What happened after their first live gig?

_____

3 ANALYSE **Find synonyms for these words in the anecdote.**

1 very good _____

2 anxious _____

3 concert _____

4 happy and enthusiastic _____

5 finish _____

4 **Match the parts of the anecdote to the correct paragraph.**

1 Details about the main event ☐

2 Conclusion: what happened / will happen in the future ☐

3 Introduction and hopes and dreams for the future ☐

4 Give background information, e.g. descriptions of people or places ☐

5 PLAN **Think of an anecdote about a real or invented positive event. Make notes about these things.**

1 set the scene

2 describe the people or place

3 describe how the event developed

4 write the ending and explain any future consequences

6 PRODUCE **Write your anecdote (200–250 words). Use your notes from Exercise 5. Make sure you include all the points in the checklist.**

✓ **CHECKLIST**

☐ Think of an interesting title.

☐ Organise your ideas in paragraphs.

☐ Use a variety of tenses.

☐ Use synonyms to make your anecdote more interesting.

☐ Check your spelling and punctuation.

LISTENING

1 🔊 7.01 **Listen and write the number of the dialogue (1–3) in the boxes.**

 a It's about someone who wants to be in the school orchestra. ☐

 b It's about someone who wants to be in a band. ☐

 c It's about someone who wants to be in the basketball team. ☐

2 🔊 7.01 **Listen again and mark the sentences T (true) or F (false).**

 1 1 Marcus will be playing in the orchestra tonight. ☐

 2 May might start piano lessons. ☐

 2 3 Matt has got a chance of being picked for the team because he's tall. ☐

 4 Luckily nobody else wants to be in the basketball team. ☐

 3 5 Jamie will not be joining the band. ☐

 6 Amanda plays the drums really well. ☐

DIALOGUE

1 **Put the sentences in order to make a dialogue.**

☐ **Simon** Don't let it get you down. Your term grades are really good. You were probably just having a bad day.

☐ **Simon** Hey, Miranda, cheer up! Things can't be that bad.

☐ **Simon** You see, there is light at the end of the tunnel.

☐ **Simon** Hang in there, Miranda. You'll pass it next time.

☐ **Miranda** Yes, they can. I've failed my Physics exam.

☐ **Miranda** Thanks, you two. You've really cheered me up.

☐ **Helena** And anyway, you've just got one more year of Physics and then you can give it up.

☐ **Helena** Yes, Simon's right. Look on the bright side, Miranda. You only failed the Physics exam. You could have failed the Chemistry and Maths exams too!

> **PRONUNCIATION**
> Intonation: encouraging someone
> Go to page 120. 🎧

PHRASES FOR FLUENCY

→ SB p.72

1 **Circle the correct options.**

> ✈ Natalie
> Natalie@thinkmail.com
>
> Hi Kate,
>
> Guess what? I've entered a competition to win a trip to Iceland. My mum warned me not to ¹*go for it / get my hopes up*. Hundreds of people enter competitions like this one. But it's not like I'll ²*make a fool of myself / go for it* or anything. My dad told me to ³*go for it / get my hopes up* anyway. Someone has to win and that someone might be me. Dad's got a very positive attitude to life. ⁴*Fair enough / Anyway*, he's always been successful, so he's got nothing to be negative about. But maybe his positivity is the reason for his success. ⁵*Anyway / Fair enough*, I've entered the competition and if I win, I want you to come to Iceland with me. If you don't try, you don't succeed and I've got nothing to lose ⁶*for a start / to make a fool of*.
>
> So fingers crossed we're off to Iceland!
>
> Love,
>
> Natalie.

2 **Complete the dialogues with phrases in Exercise 1.**

 1 **May** Are you going to tell him?

 Elena No, I don't want to be the one to tell him.

 May _____ . I expect Mr Williams will.

 2 **Elena** My piano teacher's really good. You can come and practise with me.

 May Why not? I'll _____ .

 3 **Matt** Do you reckon I've got a chance of being in the team? I've got myself really worked up about it.

 Harry You shouldn't let it get you down like this. Now, I don't want to _____ , but I think you've got a chance.

 4 **Harry** That's tall! You should get in the team – no problem. However, I know Mike and Jake want to get in the team, too.

 Matt Everyone wants to be in the basketball team and there's only one place. I don't want to _____ .

 5 **Pia** Hey, did you hear? Jamie wants to join us.

 Joe Well, he can't, Pia.

 Pia Why not?

 Joe Well, _____ , he can't play any musical instruments.

 6 **Joe** Maybe a few notes. _____ , I've already asked Amanda.

 Pia Asked her what?

READING AND USE OF ENGLISH
Part 2: Open cloze

1 For questions 1–8, read the text below and think of the word which best fits each gap. Use only one word in each gap. There is an example at the beginning (0).

Top tips for revising

Are you somebody ^{0}_____*who*_____ gets very stressed before exams? Well, a little bit of stress is a good thing because it encourages you to work hard. However, a lot of stress is not good for you: it can cause tiredness and it ^{1}_____ it harder to remember things. This means you won't be at your best when you take the exam.

Here are five tips to help you cope ^{2}_____ the stress. Firstly, eat healthily. Eat lots of fruit and vegetables and always have a good breakfast before you go to school. Don't eat too many sweets or too ^{3}_____ chocolate and don't drink cola or sugary drinks. Secondly, get lots ^{4}_____ sleep. We recommend eight to ten hours a night. Thirdly, do some exercise. Exercise helps you relax and gives you more energy, ^{5}_____ make sure you include some in your revision timetable. Fourthly, don't leave all your revision ^{6}_____ the night before the exam. You won't remember any of it in the morning and you'll feel very tired. Finally, after the exam, don't compare answers with your friends. You've finished the exam and so there is ^{7}_____ point worrying about it anymore. Keep busy and enjoy life ^{8}_____ you wait to get the results.

EXAM GUIDE:

In this part of the test, there is a cloze text with eight gaps. You must fill the gaps with the correct words to complete the text.

Read the whole text for general understanding. Remember to give yourself time to read the questions, skim the text, answer the questions, and then check at the end.

The gaps usually have to be filled with grammar words such as relative pronouns, prepositions and auxiliary verbs and occasionally with a lexical item.

Think what kind of word is missing. Is it a preposition or is it a linking word or a verb? Look at the words that come immediately before it and after it.

These are some common kinds of missing words: prepositions like *to* and *for* linking words like *or* and *but* auxiliary verbs like *was* and *will* relative pronouns like *that* and *who* question words like *what* and *where* time expressions like *for*, *ago* and *since*

8 LIST IT!

Grammar video
▶ 21

⊙ GRAMMAR
Conditionals (review) → SB p.76

1 ★☆☆ **Match the parts of the sentences.**

1 I'll put the coffee on ☐
2 If you hadn't been late, ☐
3 If my dad gets up first, ☐
4 I wouldn't post that photo on Instagram ☐
5 If you find the homework difficult, ☐
6 You'd have passed the test ☐
7 If I had the chance, ☐
8 People don't usually go by boat ☐
9 Hannah would be more popular ☐

a if I were you.
b if you'd studied harder.
c I'd go to the US.
d you'd have seen the beginning of the film.
e if they can afford the air fare.
f if I get up first.
g if she didn't say such nasty things.
h I'll help you.
i he makes breakfast.

2 ★★☆ **Complete the sentences using the prompts.**

0 If we go to Paris, / visit / the Louvre museum.
   If we go to Paris, we'll visit the Louvre
   museum.

1 If Charlie didn't work so much, / have / time / relax
   _____

2 Marco would have taken part in the race if / not break / leg
   _____

3 If people love cats, / often / not like / dogs much
   _____

4 Stefan will buy a car if / his father / lend him / money
   _____

5 Ed would ask Jenni out if / not be / so shy
   _____

6 Anna wouldn't have fallen if / see / ice / the path
   _____

3 ★★★ **Complete the sentences with the correct form of the verbs.**

0 If I _____had_____ (have) more free time,
   I ___would go___ (go) to the cinema more often.

1 If Tomoko _____ (come) to my party last night,
   she _____ (meet) my cousin.

2 Suze _____ (win) the race if she
   _____ (train) every day.

3 If people _____ (own) a car, they normally
   _____ (not use) public transport as much.

4 We _____ (visit) our grandmother more often
   if she _____ (live) closer.

5 If we _____ (see) Jonas, we
   _____ (tell) him you called.

6 You _____ (not fall) off your bike last night if
   you _____ (not ride) so fast.

7 If Joe _____ (be) older, he _____
   (be able) to see that film.

8 In general, an injection _____ (not hurt) so
   much if you _____ (relax) completely.

4 ★★★ **Complete the text with the words in the list.**

can't (x2) | 'd have (x2) | don't | had (x2)
hadn't | is | will | won't | wouldn't have

Luke is going to do his driving test. His instructor has given him a checklist of things to do when he takes his test. He said, 'Check the car seat. If the seat ¹_____ too far back, you ²_____ find it hard to reach the pedals. And if you ³_____ reach the pedals easily, you ⁴_____ drive smoothly. Check the mirrors. If you ⁵_____ look in them, you ⁶_____ see the traffic behind or beside you.' Luke just thought, 'I think I'm going to fail. Not enough lessons. If I ⁷_____ had more time, I ⁸_____ taken more lessons.'

The test was a bit of a disaster. Afterwards he spoke to his instructor. 'If I ⁹_____ remembered to check the mirrors, I ¹⁰_____ driven out into the traffic like I did. I ¹¹_____ passed if I ¹²_____ hit that wall.'

Mixed conditionals SB p.77

5 ⭐⭐⭐ **Write mixed conditional sentences about these situations.**

0 I don't have a big car. I didn't give all my friends a lift to the match.
If I had a big car, I'd have given all my friends a lift to the match.

1 I didn't read his text carefully. Now I don't know where to meet him.
_____

2 Kim didn't see the step. Now she feels really silly.
_____

3 Jordan arrived early. Now he's waiting for his friends.
_____

4 I didn't study Spanish. I can't help you with your Spanish homework.
_____

5 I left my phone at home. I don't know the way to their house.
_____

6 Monica doesn't like horror films. She didn't accept Oliver's invitation.
_____

7 Tessa didn't watch the last episode. She doesn't know the ending.
_____

8 Tim broke his leg. He is in hospital.
_____

6 ⭐⭐⭐ **Complete these mixed conditional sentences so that they are true for you.**

1 If I had _____ last week, I _____ now.
2 If I hadn't _____ last night, I wouldn't _____ now.
3 I wouldn't _____ now if I had _____ last term.
4 I would _____ now if I had _____ last year.

PRONUNCIATION
Weak forms with conditionals
Go to page 120. 🎧

7 ⭐⭐⭐ **Write a conditional sentence for each picture.**

0 *If mum liked our music, she wouldn't have complained about the noise.*

1 He _____

2 They _____
3 If he _____

GET IT RIGHT!

Conditionals
Learners often use the wrong verb form in conditional clauses.

✓ I would have remembered if I had made a list.
✗ I would have remembered if I made a list.

Correct the underlined mistake in each sentence.

1 If the police <u>didn't look</u> into the matter, the crime would never have been discovered.
_____

2 Unless we come up with some new ideas, we <u>wouldn't have</u> a chance of winning the competition.
_____

3 Davey will get the answer as long as we <u>helped</u> him.
_____

4 Suppose I did go to the party, what <u>will</u> I wear?
_____

5 Provided that the calculations were correct, the structure <u>would</u> be totally safe.
_____

6 Come to my house by 8 pm at the latest, otherwise we <u>would</u> miss the beginning of the film.
_____

73

 **VOCABULARY**
Phrasal verbs (2) → SB p.76

1 ⭐☆☆ **Make eight phrasal verbs from the table. You need to use one of the verbs twice.**

carry		
come		
pick	down	
point	out	on
run	through	with
try	up	
turn		

1 _____
2 _____
3 _____
4 _____
5 _____
6 _____
7 _____
8 _____

2 ⭐⭐☆ **Rewrite the sentences by replacing the underlined phrase with the correct form of a phrasal verb from Exercise 1.**

0 The strange noises in the night <u>were discovered</u> to be the neighbour's cat.
The strange noises in the night turned out to be the *neighbour's cat.*

1 I didn't know where the shop was until Kate <u>showed me</u> the store guide.
_____

2 The instructions for the game were really long, so we just <u>looked at</u> them quickly.
_____

3 Shall we <u>test</u> our new trainers today for the first time?
_____

4 We couldn't think of what to do until Sally <u>suddenly had</u> a brilliant idea.
_____

5 I didn't <u>become aware of</u> the differences between the two languages until I listened carefully.
_____

6 A group of volunteers are <u>making</u> repairs to people's bikes for free.
_____

7 I think we ate something bad – we all <u>got ill with</u> a stomach bug.
_____

3 ⭐⭐⭐ **Write a sentence for a time when you or someone you know …**

1 came down with something.
_____

2 came up with the solution for something.
_____

3 ran through something with someone.
_____

4 tried out something new.
_____

5 turned out to be something.
_____

6 carried something out.
_____

Alternatives to *if* → SB p.79

4 ⭐⭐☆ **Complete the sentences with one of the alternatives to *if*.**

1 We need to take the first train in the morning. _____ , we'll be late.
2 _____ Mum heard you say that! She'd be really angry!
3 You can borrow my book _____ you give it back to me tomorrow.
4 Dad said I can't go to the music festival _____ I pay for my own ticket.
5 You can get a weekend job _____ you don't work for more than five hours a day.

5 ⭐⭐⭐ **Rewrite these sentences using alternatives to *if*. Sometimes there is more than one possibility.**

1 If you didn't live here, where would you like to live?
_____

2 The teacher said I wouldn't do well if I didn't do my homework.
_____

3 OK, you can use my phone if you don't have your own.
_____

4 I have to go. If I don't, I'll miss the bus.
_____

5 Mum says we can go if we promise to be back in time for dinner.
_____

REFERENCE

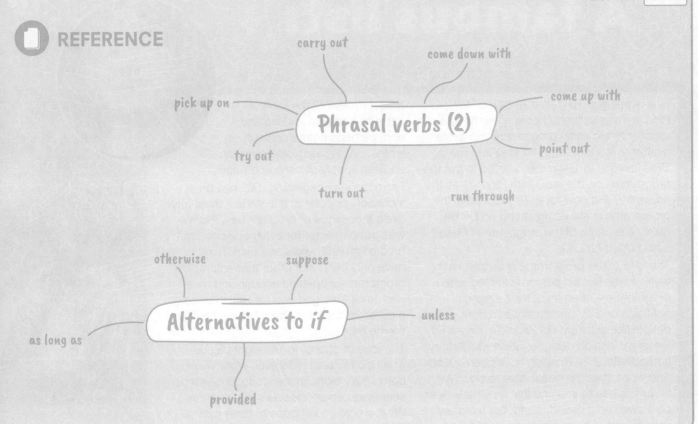

Phrasal verbs (2)

carry out
come down with
pick up on
come up with
try out
point out
turn out
run through

Alternatives to *if*

otherwise
suppose
as long as
unless
provided

VOCABULARY EXTRA

1 Read the text and find five phrasal verbs related to health and fitness.

If you don't want to join in a group exercise class at the gym, then why not design your own exercise routine that you can do at home?

The most important thing is to warm up properly before you start. Running up and down the stairs is a good way to do this.

Start with some simple weights exercises which will build up muscles. You don't need weights, use tins or bottles of water.

Even if you're feeling tired near the end, don't give up! Try and finish the exercises even if you have to go more slowly.

Then at the end, it's always good to cool down with some gentle exercises. I like lying on the floor and stretching.

2 Match the phrasal verbs in Exercise 1 with the definitions.

1 stop trying to do something before you have finished because it is difficult

_____

2 prepare yourself for physical activity by doing gentle exercises _____

3 to become involved in an activity with other people

_____

4 increase _____

5 continue to exercise gently to prevent injury after doing more difficult exercises

_____

3 Write five tips for a home-exercise routine using phrasal verbs in Exercise 1.

_____
_____
_____

A famous list:
Desert Island Discs

One evening in 1941, a man called Roy Plomley was sitting at home when he had idea for a new radio programme. He wrote a letter to the BBC with his idea and the BBC loved it. In 1942, they started to put the programme on the radio with Plomley as the presenter, and now, over 70 years later, the programme is still going strong on British radio. The name of the programme? *Desert Island Discs* (or *DID*).

The idea of the programme is simple: each week a well-known person is invited to the programme – often an actor, a singer, a politician or a TV personality. In recent years, people like actor Daniel Radcliffe, singer Ed Sheeran, fashion designer Stella McCartney and novelist J. K. Rowling have been guests. And what does the guest have to do? Well, he or she has to imagine that they have been cast away on a desert island, but that they are allowed to have eight pieces of music with them. The programme is an interview with the guest, talking about their life and work. The eight pieces of music that the guest talks about are mixed in.

After some initial programmes, the list of eight songs was added to: guests are now also allowed to choose one book and one special, luxury item to have with them on the island. Guests have had some really cool ideas. The former footballer, David Beckham,

asked to take all the football caps he had won for England and, perhaps not surprisingly, writer J. K. Rowling asked for 'an endless supply of pens and paper'.

From the very beginning, *DID* has been incredibly popular and it still is – there have been thousands of programmes. Plomley was the presenter for every episode until he died in 1985 and since then there have only been four other presenters. The programme's opening and closing music has never changed and for British people it is immediately recognisable as the *DID* theme music.

The idea of choosing just eight pieces of music to listen to forever, while you're completely alone in the world, is one that seems to capture people's imagination. What would you choose to have with you? Of course, if you like music at all, it's almost impossible to come up with a list of only eight pieces of music without leaving out things that you love. But that, perhaps, is part of the beauty of the whole *DID* concept.

DID – Did you know?

The most chosen …

- pop group and song: The Beatles, *Yesterday*
- singer and song: Frank Sinatra; *My Way*
- novelist: Charles Dickens
- classical composer: Mozart
- luxury: pianos, guitars and binoculars

READING

1 **Look at the title of the article and the photos. Read the article quickly. What do these words refer to?**

> eight | luxury | imagination | well-known

2 **Read the article again and answer the questions.**

1 How did Desert Island Discs start?
_____

2 Who are the guests on the programme?
_____

3 What ten things can guests take with them to the island?
_____

4 How many presenters have there been?
_____

5 What is the difficult part of making a list of eight pieces of music?
_____

3 CRITICAL THINKING **Imagine you are going to live on a desert island. Put the items below in order of importance for you (1 = most important). Which are necessary for your physical and mental survival? Then add two more of your own.**

> a family member ☐ | a football pitch ☐
> a microwave ☐ | games and puzzles ☐
> a laptop/phone/tablet/games console ☐
> fresh food ☐ | wi-fi ☐
> your best friend ☐

4 **Imagine you could be a guest on *DID*. What eight pieces of music would you choose? What would your book and your luxury item be? Write a short paragraph (60–80 words).**

DEVELOPING *Writing*

Advice for travelling – an email

1 **INPUT** **Read the emails quickly and answer the questions.**

1 What is the climate of Laura's holiday destination?
_____

2 What five items of clothing does Sawyer suggest taking?
_____

3 What three essential items does he suggest taking?
_____

Laura
Laura@thinkmail.com

Hi Sawyer,
Guess what? I'm going to northern Sweden this winter, so it's going to be really cold, maybe wet, too. I'm looking forward to the trip, but I'm really not very sure what I should take. Living here in Istanbul, where the weather is usually warm and sunny, means I'm not very good at winter packing! I know you've done lots of travelling and been to hot and cold places. 🙂
Can you help?
Laura

Sawyer
Sawyer@thinkmail.com

Hi Laura,
Great to hear from you. That's so exciting about your trip – it'll be so different for you, not like home! But you're right, it's important to think about what to take. OK, well the first thing of course is clothes, obviously!
A hat is the best protection against the cold, but you'll need to wear it – don't leave it in your suitcase. If you've got one that covers your ears, then even better!
Sweaters and coats are good, but it's better to think about wearing several layers of thin clothing rather than single, heavy items.
Take at least one good pair of waterproof shoes. You don't want wet, cold feet!
Don't forget a pair of gloves – they're always a good idea – as long as they're light and waterproof.
There are other things that some people might not think are essentials, but if I were you, I'd take:
• a pair of sunglasses. If you're going to be out and about in the snow, you'll definitely need to protect your eyes from the bright reflection of the snow.
• some sunscreen. I know, sunscreen in winter seems wrong, doesn't it? You'll be surprised, though, how the wind can burn your skin, so you'll need good protection.
• lip balm. This will help stop your lips getting sore from the wind and cold.
Hope this helps but just let me know if you need any more tips 🙂 When do you leave?
Have a great holiday!
Sawyer

2 **Read Sawyer's email again and answer the questions.**

1 What's the best kind of hat to take?
_____

2 What's better than a single, heavy sweater?
_____

3 What should the shoes protect you from?
_____

4 Why should you take sunglasses in winter?
_____

5 How can you protect your lips?
_____

3 **ANALYSE** **Answer the questions about the email.**

1 How does Sawyer introduce his reply?
_____

2 How does he separate out the different things he suggests taking?
_____

3 How does Sawyer indicate reasons for what to take?
_____

4 **PLAN** **You are going to write an email to a friend who wants advice about what to take on holiday. Read what the friend writes. Choose a or b for your answer. Then make notes in the table about the things you are going to tell them and the reasons.**

Javi
Javi@thinkmail.com

Hi …
I'm going on holiday to **a)** a really hot place **b)** your town/city. But I'm not sure what to take with me. Can you give me a nice, simple list of ideas please?
Thanks!
Javi

Idea	Reason

5 **PRODUCE** **Write your reply (200–250 words). Use your answer from Exercise 4 and your notes. Make sure you include all the points in the checklist.**

 CHECKLIST

☐ Start with a short introduction.
☐ Use bullet points for your list.
☐ Consider clothes and other essential items.
☐ For each thing, give a reason for taking it.

 **LISTENING**

1 🔊 8.02   **Listen to Ari, Bella and Colin talking. Complete the information.**

Three things I couldn't live without

Colin

1 Phone

2 _____

3 _____

Bella

1 _____

2 _____

3 _____

Ari

1 _____

2 _____

3 _____

2 🔊 8.02   **Listen again. Mark the statements T (true), F (false) or DS (doesn't say).**

1 Their friend Flora has gone away for a weekend with her parents. ☐

2 Flora isn't happy that she can't take her phone. ☐

3 Colin realises he doesn't need his e-reader if he's got his phone. ☐

4 Bella's third choice is based on the fact that she likes the colour blue. ☐

5 Ari thinks it's sad if you can only think of three things you can't live without. ☐

6 Bella doesn't like serious discussions. ☐

7 Ari doesn't accept Colin's first idea for his third thing. ☐

8 Colin considers himself to be a good guitar player. ☐

3 **Write your list of three things that you couldn't live without. Explain why.**

1 _____
  _____

2 _____
  _____

3 _____
  _____

DIALOGUE

1 **Put the sentences in order to make dialogues.**

1 ☐ **Adam** Like the way that guy last night did? I think if I was a contestant on that programme, I'd have shouted at him.

  ☐ **Adam** But do you think you would behave better? I mean, in a situation like that.

  ☐ **Adam** Are you watching that reality show about people stuck on an island?

  ☐ **Adam** He certainly will. Well, unless one of the other people starts behaving even worse.

  ☐ **Briony** Good question. And you know, I think I'd be OK, as long as the other people didn't make me angry.

  ☐ **Briony** Yes, I think it's great. I love watching people behaving badly!

  ☐ **Briony** And that's always a possibility, right? Listen, why don't we watch the next episode together?

  ☐ **Briony** Me too. He was awful. If he carries on like that, he'll be voted off next week.

2 ☐ **Lois** Of course I will, don't worry. Why wouldn't I look after it?

  ☐ **Lois** Not true. I looked after it. I just gave it back later than I'd promised.

  ☐ **Lois** Can I borrow your tablet?

  ☐ **Lois** Of course I would have. But OK, don't lend me the tablet. I don't mind.

  ☐ **Noah** No, it's OK. You can borrow it. Otherwise you'll never talk to me again. Just joking, Lois!

  ☐ **Noah** Why? Well, I remember you didn't really look after the camera I lent you.

  ☐ **Noah** Well, yes, I suppose so – as long as you promise to look after it.

  ☐ **Noah** Right. And if I hadn't reminded you, you'd never have given it back.

2 **Choose one of the situations. Write a dialogue between the two people (6–8 lines).**

1 Elena wants Amy to go shopping with her. Amy remembers previous shopping experiences with Elena, that weren't very good. In the end, Amy agrees.

2 Ben wants to go and see a concert. His parents will only let him go if a friend goes, too. Ben's friend Sam doesn't really like listening to music at concerts.

B2 First for Schools

EXAM GUIDE:

In Part 1 of the B2 First for Schools Listening exam, you will listen to eight different recordings. Each recording is either a short monologue, or a short dialogue. You have to answer one three-option multiple-choice question about each recording. The questions don't always focus on the same aspects of the recording, however. They can be about the text as a whole, or about a detail from the text. They can be about the purpose of the text, or about the opinion of the speaker(s). It is important to read the questions carefully before you listen so that you know what to listen for. You will hear each recording twice.

- Read both the question itself and the three options before you listen.
- Remember to listen for synonyms, paraphrases and expressions with similar meanings, as you will not hear the exact same words as in the options.

1 ◁)) 8.03 **You will hear people talking in eight different situations.**
For questions 1–8, choose the best answer (A, B or C).

1 You hear a critic reviewing a new novel.
What is her criticism of the novel?
A The plot is rather predictable.
B The action in it is too slow.
C The people in it are difficult to like.

2 You hear two friends talking about playing the guitar.
What is the boy doing?
A reassuring the girl about her ability
B persuading the girl to help him get better
C describing something he learnt to the girl

3 You hear two friends talking about a class trip to a science exhibition.
What do they agree about?
A The interactive displays were interesting.
B There were some surprising displays.
C It had fewer displays than they were expecting.

4 You hear a young singer talking about becoming successful.
What is she surprised about?
A how little free time she now gets
B how many interviews she's asked to do
C how often she's recognised in the street

5 You hear two friends talking about entering a talent show.
How does the boy feel about entering it?
A optimistic about doing well in it
B willing to learn from the experience
C curious about the other competitors

6 You hear two friends talking about their local sports centre.
The girl thinks that it should
A employ more highly qualified staff.
B be cheaper for young people to use.
C offer a wider range of sports.

7 You hear a teacher talking about some homework.
Why is he talking to the class?
A to change a deadline for the homework
B to add an extra task to the homework
C to suggest more reference sources for the homework

8 You hear part of a discussion programme about the environment.
What topic are they talking about?
A cleaning up plastic in seas
B reducing the use of plastic
C improving the recycling of plastic

CONSOLIDATION

🎧 LISTENING

1 🔊 8.04 **Listen to Dario and Maddie. Tick (✓) the things that Maddie is taking with her on holiday.**

2 🔊 8.04 **Listen again and answer the questions.**

1 What negative things does Maddie talk about with regard to camping?

_____

2 Why are tablets for stomachache on her list?

_____

3 Why does Dario agree that it's a good idea for Maddie to take medicines with her?

_____

4 What condition did Maddie's parents state for her taking her tablet with her?

_____

5 What does Dario say that makes Maddie panic?

_____

6 What does Dario say about the next time they see each other?

_____

 GRAMMAR

3 **Circle the correct options.**

1 I'm going to have a shower as soon as I *get / will get* home.
2 If I spoke another language as well as you do, I'*d be / was* really pleased with myself.
3 If you *don't / won't* help me, I'll be really angry with you.
4 By the time you read this, I *will have arrived / will have been arriving* in the US.
5 I can't see you tomorrow night – we *go / are going* to my uncle's birthday party.
6 If you'd told us where you were going, we *wouldn't be / wouldn't have been* so upset now.
7 This time tomorrow, we'll *watch / be watching* my sister's first appearance on TV.
8 By next year we *will live / will have lived* in this flat for more than ten years.

🅰🆉 VOCABULARY

4 **Match the parts of the sentences.**

1 Our weekend was ruined when my best friend came ☐
2 I've got a really good feeling ☐
3 She's decided she wants to carry ☐
4 Everything will be fine unless ☐
5 We weren't sure what to do, but Sue came ☐
6 We'd better go now, otherwise ☐
7 It isn't easy to work ☐
8 Let's just take a moment, please, and run ☐

a up with a brilliant idea.
b we get home really late.
c down with a really bad cold.
d about the game tonight.
e through the names again.
f out the research, no matter what.
g we'll be late getting home.
h out why that happened.

5 **Complete the missing words.**

1 Can I just p_____ out that this isn't your first mistake.
2 We're all looking f_____ to seeing you again.
3 I hate camping, so I'm really d_____ this weekend!
4 I don't care what you do, p_____ you don't get me into trouble.
5 Don't worry about it. We can r_____ everything again before the performance.
6 I'm not sure about our new house, but my parents feel quite p_____ about moving there.
7 We got to the address on time, but it t_____ out to be the wrong place.
8 I guess it'll be OK, but I'm a bit a_____ about tomorrow's test.

DIALOGUE

6 Complete the dialogue with the phrases in the list. There are three you don't need.

> anyway | cheer up | for a start
> fair enough | get my hopes up
> go for it | I think so | so far | so-so

Paul So what happened at your interview? Oh, you look pretty unhappy. How did it go?

Annie ¹_____ . Lots of things went wrong. I was late ²_____ .

Paul Oh dear. Were they angry about that?

Annie ³_____ . Well, they certainly didn't smile much. And the woman who was the main interviewer said they could only give me 15 minutes.

Paul ⁴_____ , I suppose.

Annie Yes, you're right. After all, they have other things to do. ⁵_____ , they asked me some questions, but I don't think I answered them especially well.

Paul Well, ⁶_____ . If you don't get the job, you can try other places.

Annie But there aren't any other places! Oh well, I'll just have to wait until they contact me, I suppose.

READING

7 Read the article and answer the questions.

1 What are the origins of FOMO?

_____

2 What is the difference between FOMO and JOMO?

_____

3 How can accepting FOMO help?

_____

4 Why is it important to understand your feelings?

_____

5 How can you feel more control of FOMO?

_____

6 What can happen if you compare your own life to other people's all the time?

_____

WRITING

8 Write Step 5 (80–100 words) for the article on how to avoid FOMO.

FOMO OR JOMO?

FOMO, the 'fear of missing out', is not a new problem. In fact, it dates back to when people lived in groups. If one group found a new food source and another one didn't, they would feel they had missed out. This could mean the difference between life and death.

Nowadays, FOMO is when you feel apprehensive about other people having a better time than you when you are not with them, but it isn't a matter of life or death. It's not just the feeling that there might be better or more interesting things that you could be doing, it's the feeling that you're missing out on something important that friends are experiencing right now. This can result in feeling stressed.

JOMO, on the other hand, is the joy of missing out. It's a feeling of happiness with yourself and your own activities without being really worried about missing out on what other people might be doing. If you want to turn FOMO into JOMO and you're a bit unsure about how or where to start, try to work through these four simple steps.

---

1 Accept your feelings of FOMO.
No one likes feeling left out and you shouldn't feel ashamed to admit that. Instead of rejecting FOMO, why not accept your feelings and try to change them? Accept how you feel, so the next time it happens, you'll be able to pick up on how you're feeling more quickly and then start to recognise it.

---

2 Be curious.
Check in with yourself and find out exactly what's going on with your feelings. If you ask yourself some questions, maybe you'll come up with some answers or explanations. Do you care more about the activity your friends are doing without you or is it more about not being part of the group? If you missed the activity, then you could try and do it the next week. If you feel like your friends are excluding you, then why not find a different friend or group?

---

3 Face your FOMO.
The more we try to avoid something, the more it appears. It's the same with FOMO. Instead of pretending your FOMO doesn't exist, listen to the feeling and get to know it better. Don't dread it. Try and feel positive about it. Once you've recognised the feeling, you'll gradually feel more in control of it.

---

4 Live in the moment.
Look around you and be happy and grateful for the people and things you have in your life right here, right now. Make an effort to stop comparing yourself to other people and their lives and try not to miss out on your own life.

So next time FOMO pays you a visit, try and turn it into JOMO – it might turn out to be the best decision you've ever made!

9 TAKE CHARGE

Grammar video ▶24

GRAMMAR

I wish and *If only* → SB p.86

1 ★☆☆ **Read the sentences. Does the person regret their present situation or do they regret a past action? Write PA (past) or PR (present).**

1 If only I didn't have so much homework. ☐
2 I wish I had said what I felt. ☐
3 If only I'd gone to bed earlier. ☐
4 I wish I could speak French. ☐
5 If only I hadn't said anything. ☐
6 I wish Owen would call. ☐

2 ★★☆ **Complete the sentences with the correct form of the verbs in the list.**

> be | get | help | let | listen
> not get | understand | work

1 I wish my dad would _____ to me.
2 If only he _____ what it's like to be a teenager.
3 I wish he had _____ me go to the party.
4 I wish I hadn't _____ so angry with him.
5 If only I could _____ him.
6 I wish he _____ so angry.
7 If only I had _____ less strict when he was a child.
8 I wish I hadn't _____ so much when he was younger.

3 ★★☆ **Complete the sentences using the correct form of the words in brackets.**

1 I don't feel very well. _____
   I _____ so much. (If only / not eat)
2 You have to be 18 to watch this film.
   _____ I _____ so young. (wish / not be)
3 Holly's so complicated. _____
   I _____ what she was thinking. (wish / know)
4 I don't know how to do this homework.
   _____ I _____ attention in class today. (If only / pay)
5 I can't hear a thing today. _____
   I _____ to that concert last night. (wish / not go)
6 I'm not good enough to get in the school team.
   _____ I _____ football better. (wish / play)
7 I really wanted to see that film. I _____
   you _____ me the ending. (wish / not tell)
8 We've still got one more hour of school.
   _____ we _____ home now. (If only / can go)

4 ★★★ **Read the sentences and write one past regret and one present regret for each one.**

0 I've got a really bad headache.
   I wish I could go home. If only I hadn't spent all night playing on the computer.
1 My sister plays her music really loud.
   _____
2 I haven't got any money.
   _____
3 We've got a Maths test today.
   _____
4 My computer's broken.
   _____

PRONUNCIATION
Intrusive /w/ and /j/ Go to page 120. 🎧

I would prefer to ..., It's time, I'd rather / sooner

→ SB p.89

5 ★☆☆ **Circle the correct options.**

1 I would rather you *don't / didn't* ask so many questions. I'm tired.

2 I'd prefer *to invite / inviting* George than Henry.

3 It's time Natalia *starts / started* behaving more like an adult.

4 Would you prefer it if we *take / took* a break for five minutes?

5 I'd sooner *spend / spent* the money on a new TV.

6 I'd prefer it if they *don't / didn't* come this evening.

7 We'd sooner you *don't / didn't* let your dog come into our garden.

8 It's time someone *takes / took* this problem seriously.

6 ★★☆ **Complete the dialogue with the correct form of the verbs in brackets.**

Anna Dan. It's time we ¹_____ a talk. (have)

Dan Really? Now? I'd prefer ²_____ TV. (watch)

Anna That's the problem. You never want to talk.

Dan OK, we can talk but can't it wait? I'd rather we ³_____ after this film. (talk)

Anna And I'd sooner we ⁴_____ now. (chat)

Dan What is it? Make it quick, please.

Anna OK. Can I have the remote?

Dan The remote?

Anna Yes, the remote control.

Dan OK, here you are, but why do you want it?

Anna Because I'd prefer we ⁵_____ the news. (watch)

Dan Hey, I was watching that film!

7 ★★★ **Complete the second sentence so it has a similar meaning to the first using the word given. Use between two and five words including the word given.**

1 Play tennis or volleyball? Tennis is my choice. **PREFER**
   I _____ tennis.

2 You need to learn to ride a bike. **TIME**
   It's _____ to ride a bike.

3 The film starts too late. I can't watch it. **DIDN'T**
   If _____ start so late.

4 I'd prefer to eat at home. **WE**
   I'd rather _____ at home.

5 I told Dad a lie. That was a mistake. **WISH**
   I _____ Dad a lie.

6 Can we go to France this year, rather than Italy?
   PREFER
   I _____ we went to France this year.

7 Someone needs to tell her. **TOLD**
   It's _____ her.

GET IT RIGHT!

would rather / would prefer

Learners often use the wrong verb form after *would rather* or *would prefer*.

✓ They would rather say ...

✗ They would rather to say ...

✓ I'd prefer to go on holiday.

✗ I'd prefer go on holiday.

Complete the sentences with *would rather* or *would prefer*.

1 I _____ leave school and get a job than go to university.

2 Jo _____ to sleep on it and decide in the morning.

3 We _____ you weren't so unreasonable.

4 _____ you _____ start your degree course now or have a gap year?

5 Olivia _____ to have a lie in tomorrow morning if that's OK.

6 Josh _____ play tennis than watch a film.

Az VOCABULARY
Life's ups and downs → SB p.86

1 ⭐⭐☆ **Complete the rules with the words in the list.**

> blame | dwell | get | go
> let | tricky | way | work

Five
little rules of life

1 Don't always _____ someone else when things don't _____ your way.

2 Don't let the little things _____ in the way of the important stuff.

3 Don't _____ on things too long when they don't _____ out well.

4 If you feel that someone has _____ you down, try not to worry about it. Move on.

5 If something is _____ for you to deal with or things don't work out the _____ you'd like them to, stay positive.

2 ⭐⭐☆ **Which of the rules in Exercise 1 should these people follow?**

1 'Why did I fail the test? Why? I should have studied harder. I shouldn't have gone out last weekend. I'm going to regret not taking it more seriously for the rest of my life.' ☐

2 'The referee was terrible. He clearly wanted the other side to win and made all his decisions to ensure that they did.' ☐

3 'It's so hard training for the race and I'm finding it really difficult. I feel like giving up.' ☐

4 'I can't get started on my revision until I've got my room tidied and answered all my emails.' ☐

5 'I can't believe Jamie didn't come to my party. He promised he would. And it's not the first time. I wish I'd never asked him.' ☐

Work and education → SB p.87

3 ⭐☆☆ **Unscramble the letters to make eight words or expressions about work and education.**

1 greede _____
2 thapinpricesep _____
3 rescare voraisd _____
4 cohols reveal _____
5 orwk nepixeerec _____
6 file epierecexn _____
7 degrauat _____
8 naluch ruyo won sneusbis _____

4 ⭐⭐☆ **Complete the sentences with the correct form of words and expressions in Exercise 3.**

1 Get a Saturday job. It's good to try and get a bit of _____ while you're still at school.

2 My _____ is in journalism.

3 If you want to _____ , you need a great idea and a lot of money.

4 There aren't so many good jobs for _____ these days because so many people are going to university.

5 More and more _____ are going to university these days.

6 I think _____ is more important than education.

7 We're doing an _____ instead of going to university.

8 I had no idea what I wanted to do after I left school, so I went to see a _____ .

5 ⭐⭐⭐ **What do you plan to do when you leave school? Write a short text (50 words) and use at least four of the phrases from Exercise 3.**

_____
_____
_____
_____

 **REFERENCE**

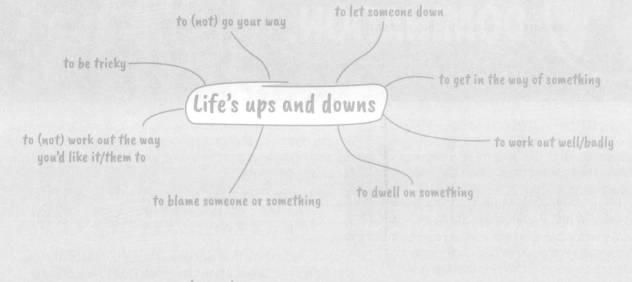

Life's ups and downs
- to (not) go your way
- to let someone down
- to be tricky
- to get in the way of something
- to (not) work out the way you'd like it/them to
- to work out well/badly
- to blame someone or something
- to dwell on something

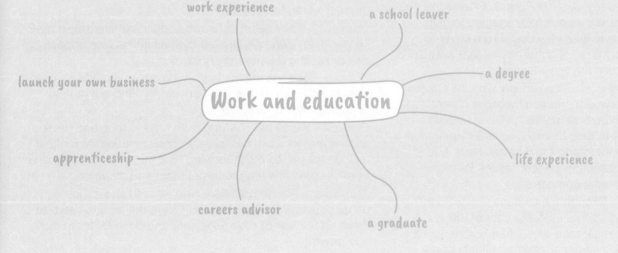

Work and education
- work experience
- a school leaver
- launch your own business
- a degree
- apprenticeship
- life experience
- careers advisor
- a graduate

 VOCABULARY EXTRA

1 Match the idioms with the definitions.

> to be as easy as ABC
> to drop out | to hit the books
> to pass with flying colours
> to put your thinking cap on
> to skip class

1 to pass with excellent results
_____

2 to not go to school or class when you're supposed to
_____

3 to be extremely easy
_____

4 to stop going to classes before you have finished the course
_____

5 to study in a serious and determined way _____

6 to think seriously about something
_____

2 Complete the dialogue with the correct form of the idioms in Exercise 1.

A Did Dani ¹_____ yesterday? I didn't see him.

B I don't know. Maybe he's decided to ²_____ already.

A No, I don't think so. He might be ill.

B Maybe or perhaps he's ³_____ .

A He did say he wanted to ⁴_____ this year.

B I'm not sure I'm going to be able to do that, so I don't know how Dani will do it.

A Yes, you can. Revising is ⁵_____ .

B Can you help me find the best ways to revise then?

A Sure, just let me ⁶_____ . First, we need to work out the kind of learner you are.

3 Answer the questions.

1 What is as easy as ABC for you?
_____

2 How often do you hit the books?
_____

3 When was the last time you put your thinking cap on?
_____

THE TEEN'S GUIDE TO
WORLD DOMINATION:

Advice on Life, Liberty, and the Pursuit of Awesomeness by Josh Shipp

It's no secret that the teenage years can be tough. But despite the difficulties, they are also potentially some of the most thrilling times of our lives. They are the times when we discover all the amazing things that we are capable of and start to make them happen. They are the beginning of our journey into life as an adult. As with other long and exciting journeys what we need is a guide to help us through it. *The Teen's Guide to World Domination: Advice on Life, Liberty, and the Pursuit of Awesomeness* is exactly that: a book for teenagers to help them achieve their very best. From cover to cover, it is full of insightful advice that will inspire and entertain anyone who reads it.

The author Josh Shipp knows what he's talking about. He was a problem teenager himself, but these days he makes his living helping teenagers to help themselves and helping their parents understand them better. He is also a regular contributor on teen issues for many different media companies.

To help us through the teenage years, Josh introduces us to a colourful cast of villains which we must face and defeat before we can reach the 'awesomeness' that all teenagers are capable of. If we want to achieve our true potential, these are some of the obstacles that might try and get in our way.

Vampires – All those bad things in life that you find yourself attracted to even though you know they are bad. Stop them from trying to lead you the wrong way and learn how to stay far away from them.

Robots – The people in your life who want to control you. They want to see you do the same things they do. Break free from their programming and find your own path through life.

Ninjas – You think they are your friends but really, they're just using you to get what they want. Don't be fooled by them. It's time to fight back.

Puppies – They seem cute and cuddly, but are they really? Look closer. Don't be blinded by their immediate appeal. Beware of the danger they hold.

Pirates – The mean kids in life who make your life a misery. There's no room for them in your world. Find out how to keep them out of your life.

Ghosts – We all get it wrong from time to time and these are the memories of mistakes you have made that make it difficult for you to move forward. But you need to break free from the past. It's time to forget them and move on.

Zombies – The complainers who want to share their unhappiness with you. You don't have the time to listen to them. Stay clear of their negativity and don't let them bring you down.

So, if you want to improve the quality of your life and dominate your world forever, make the right choices, keep good friends and find your inner hero!

📖 READING

1 **Read the book review. Who are the 'villains' that the author introduces and what should the reader do with them?**

2 **Read the review again. Mark the sentences true (T), false (F) or doesn't say (DS)?**

   1 According to Josh Shipp, the teenage years aren't always easy. ☐

   2 Josh knows what he is talking about because he was a perfect teenager. ☐

   3 Josh's book has sold millions of copies all over the world. ☐

   4 Josh's job now involves a lot of travel. ☐

   5 According to Josh, villains are like the different types of people that teenagers have to deal with. ☐

   6 According to Josh's villains, all parents are robots. ☐

3 **CRITICAL THINKING** **Think about the 'villains' in the text. Which 'villains' are these people talking about? Why?**

   1 My dad wants me to be a doctor, just like him.
   _____

   2 The last time I had to stand in front of the class and talk I made a fool of myself. I never want to do it again.
   _____

   3 Jenny Wilson says that life is never fair. I always feel depressed when I hang out with her.
   _____

   4 I've got a feeling that Bobby only likes coming over to my house because he likes my sister. _____

   5 I waste far too much time on video games. I wish I could stop playing them all the time. _____

   6 Robbie Dawson is a bully. I'm scared to go to school because I know he's there waiting for me.
   _____

4 **Choose one of the 'villains' and write a short text to describe this person or thing (60–80 words).**

DEVELOPING ✑ *Writing*

An essay about teenage life

1 **INPUT** **Read the essay. What three things would the writer like his school to offer?**

_____

Home	About	New posts		🔍

What could schools do to make life easier for teenagers?

1 The school I go to has a clear aim: to help its students achieve the best grades they can so that they can leave school with the qualifications they need for the next stage of their lives. I expect this is true of most schools around the country.

2 While this is certainly a very useful intention, it doesn't really take into consideration that teenagers are more than just empty beings to fill with information. There are many more important issues that young adults need to address other than just learning the facts. We need help in learning how to deal with conflict at school and at home. We need to be able to talk about how our emotions affect us. We need to be given information about what opportunities we will have when we leave school. Sadly, our school offers very little help in these areas.

3 Of course, I know it's asking a lot to expect schools to deal with all this on top of their academic responsibilities, but there are things they could do to help make a difference. First and foremost, I'd like to see a dedicated welfare officer, someone on hand throughout the school day to talk students through any problems they might be facing. Secondly, I'd love it if our school had a careers office, a place where you could find out what life is really like in the working world. This would certainly be useful in helping us make more informed decisions when we leave. Finally, it would be good to see a mentoring scheme, a system in which each first-year student has a 'friend' in one of the top years to show them around. This would help make the transition from primary school to secondary school a lot smoother.

4 I accept that a school's role is primarily to educate, but I'm sure I'm sure that it wouldn't take too much to implement these ideas and make our lives just a little bit easier.

2 **ANALYSE** **Choose four sentences from the essay that could be cut to shorten it.**

3 **Complete these sentences from the essay.**

1 I'd like to see a dedicated welfare officer, _____ on hand throughout …

2 I'd love it if our school had a careers office, _____ where you could find out …

3 It would be good to see a mentoring scheme, _____ in which each first-year …

4 **PLAN** **Read the essay again and complete the mind maps with the information and the paragraph where you find it.**

Important teen issues (non-educational)

Things school could offer

5 **Add three more ideas of your own to the mind maps in Exercise 4.**

6 **Write your answer to the essay question (200–250 words). Use your notes from Exercises 4 and 5.**

Write your own checklist.

✔ CHECKLIST
- ☐ _____
- ☐ _____
- ☐ _____
- ☐ _____

1 🔊 9.02   **Listen to the dialogues. Match the names Felix, Rob or Jack with the things they are complaining about.**

1 _____

2 _____

3 _____

2 🔊 9.02   **Listen again and answer the questions.**

1 What is Lucy using Felix's tablet for?

_____

2 Why isn't she using her own tablet?

_____

3 What did Lydia want to ask Rob?

_____

4 Why is Rob angry with Lydia?

_____

5 Why does Jack want Emily to keep the music down?

_____

6 What does Emily agree to do?

_____

3 🔊 9.02   **Put the words in order to make lines from the dialogue. Listen again and check.**

1 tablet / rather / without / you / I'd / take / my / asking / didn't

_____

2 off / room / you / my / took / I'd / shoes / walked / before / your / into / you / sooner

_____

3 too / it / door / shut / if / you / kept / I'd / prefer / your

_____

DIALOGUE

1 **Put the sentences in order to make a dialogue.**

☐ **Paula** A meal – that's a really good idea. Chinese or Indian?

☐ **Paula** Well, we've got to do something. How about going shopping?

☐ **Paula** OK, Italian it is. Shall I invite Fiona and Olivia?

☐ **Paula** So we've passed our exams. What are we going to do to celebrate?

☐ **Paula** OK, no problem. So let's go to the cinema.

☐ **Ruby** I'd rather not. There isn't really anything I want to buy.

☐ **Ruby** I'd prefer to try out that new Italian on Hope Street.

☐ **Ruby** That's a good question. I haven't really thought about it.

☐ **Ruby** No, I'd rather just go with you.

☐ **Ruby** I'd sooner go out for a meal.

2 **Complete the dialogues with your own ideas.**

1 **A** Would you like to watch some TV?
   B I'd prefer _____

2 **A** How about organising a party for the end of the school year?
   B I'd sooner _____

3 **A** Let's take the bus to Gran's.
   B I'd rather _____

3 **Choose an opening line and write a short dialogue (8–10 lines). Use an example of** *I'd prefer*, *I'd rather* **and** *I'd sooner*.

• 'What shall we do tonight?'
• 'What do you want to do this weekend?'
• 'Where do you want to go on holiday this summer?'

_____

_____

_____

_____

B2 First for Schools

EXAM GUIDE:

In this part of the exam you hear an interview with someone or an exchange between two people. You hear each extract twice.

- On the exam paper there are seven multiple-choice questions each with three possible answers. You have to choose the correct answer.
- Before you listen, read through the questions and options to prepare yourself for the kind of things you will hear. Read the questions carefully so you know exactly what they are looking for.
- You will need to listen out for attitudes, opinions, purpose, feelings, main points and details.
- The wrong options will often contain similar information to what you hear. They will also often contain words and phrases from the listening. Be careful because this doesn't mean they are correct.
- Use your second listening to confirm answers you have already chosen and answer those questions you weren't able to the first time.

1　🔊 9.03　**You will hear an interview with Abby Jones talking about her gap year before going to university. For questions 1–7 choose the best answer (A, B or C).**

1　Why didn't Abby go straight from school to university?

A She never thought her exams would be good enough to get her into university.

B She waited too long to make a decision.

C She changed her mind about what career she wanted to do.

2　Why was Abby a little frightened about taking a year off?

A She thought she'd lose contact with her friends.

B She felt she might not find employment when she finally finished university.

C She had no idea what to do with all that time.

3　Why didn't Abby want to spend her year off working for the police?

A As a volunteer she wouldn't get paid.

B It might put her off her dream job.

C She realised the year off was an opportunity to experience something new.

4　Why did Abby's dad mention Thailand to her?

A He had a relative out there.

B He thought she could get a job in a hotel there.

C He knew it was somewhere she'd always wanted to go.

5　What did Abby do with the money she earned?

A She used it to pay back her parents for the plane ticket.

B She gave some to her dad's cousin for letting her stay there.

C She saved it so she could go travelling.

6　What did Abby study in Thailand?

A how to cook Thai food

B how to speak Thai

C how to teach English

7　What advice does Abby offer school leavers who want to take a year out?

A You should stay close to home.

B You should go on lots of adventures.

C You should think carefully about what you're going to do.

10 UNBELIEVABLE NEWS

Grammar video

G GRAMMAR
Reported speech (review) → SB p.94

1 ⭐☆☆ **Rewrite the sentences as reported speech.**

0 'Charlie is late,' said Jo.
Jo / said / that / Charlie / be / late
Jo said that Charlie was late.

1 'I like horror stories,' said Matt.
Matt / said / that / he / like / horror / stories
_____

2 'I will see you at the concert on Saturday,' said Ali.
Ali / said / that / he / see / us / at / the concert / on Saturday
_____

3 'I have been to Spain many times,' said Helena.
Helena / said / that / she / be / to / Spain / many times
_____

4 'I'm looking forward to seeing you,' said Elif.
Elif / said / that / she / look forward / to / seeing / me
_____

2 ⭐⭐☆ **Rewrite Jamie's text messages in reported speech.**

1 I'll see you all at Jake's birthday party on Saturday.
Jamie said that _____

2 It's half-time. Our team has scored two goals.
Jamie said that _____

3 I can't get tickets for the concert. It's sold out.
Jamie said that _____

4 We aren't playing Sunnyhill School. They've cancelled the match.
Jamie said that _____

5 My Maths teacher quit yesterday. I can't believe it.
Jamie said that _____

6 I haven't done enough revision for the History exam.
Jamie said that _____

3 ⭐⭐⭐ **Read the statements from an article about Twitter. Then report them.**

1 It took three years, two months and a day to go from the first tweet to the billionth.
2 The most popular emoji on Twitter is the face with tears of joy 😂.
3 Twitter is available in 33 languages now.
4 Every month, more than 33 million people use Twitter actively.
5 Barack Obama has the most Twitter followers – more than 120 million.
6 In November 2017, Twitter expanded the character limit from 140 to 280 characters.
7 Twitter has become the fastest way to break news.
8 Snapchat will become more popular than Twitter in the future.

The article said that …
1 _____
2 _____
3 _____
4 _____
5 _____
6 _____
7 _____
8 _____

4 ⭐⭐⭐ **Report five messages you tweeted or texted this week.**
1 _____
2 _____
3 _____
4 _____
5 _____

Reported questions and requests

→ SB p.95

5 ★★☆ **Report the questions. Use + if, + to or + question word.**

0 'Do you want to be a journalist when you leave school?'

I asked her if she wanted to be a journalist when she left school.

1 'Why do you want to be a journalist?'

My friend asked me

_____

2 'Think of a name for the school online magazine.'

My teacher asked me

_____

3 'Interview a foreign correspondent for the school magazine.'

The editor of the school magazine asked me

_____

4 'Prepare some questions for the interview.'

She asked me

_____

5 'Which countries have you reported from?'

I asked the foreign correspondent, Jeremy Hope,

_____

6 'Have you reported from any war zones?'

I asked him

_____

7 'Can you get me a glass of water?'

She asked me

_____

6 ★★☆ **Match the parts of the sentences.**

1 The journalist apologised ☐
2 The police officer warned the driver ☐
3 The driver regretted ☐
4 The journalist agreed ☐
5 The public criticised the newspaper ☐
6 The director of the company accused the journalist ☐
7 The man denied ☐
8 The newspaper admitted ☐

a leaving his vehicle.
b to interview the witness.
c of upsetting his staff.
d robbing the bank.
e for upsetting the girl.
f not to leave his vehicle.
g to printing incorrect facts.
h for printing incorrect facts.

7 ★★☆ **Circle the correct options.**

1 Daisy regretted *for telling / telling* her story to the newspaper.

2 The pop star accused the newspaper *of printing / printing* lies about him.

3 The media criticised the politician *for failing / to fail* to explain his actions.

4 The film star apologised *for being / of being* late for the interview.

5 The victim's wife agreed *speaking / to speak* to the press.

6 The boy admitted to *drive / driving* the car without a licence.

7 The bank manager admitted *to make / that he had made* a mistake.

8 The boy was warned *about entering / for entering* the empty building.

8 ★★★ **Now write sentences that are for you.**

1 I regret _____

2 I apologised _____

3 I admit _____

4 My mum/dad/friend warned me _____

5 I agreed _____

GET IT RIGHT!

say and *tell* in reported speech

Learners often make mistakes with *say* and *tell*.

✓ I told Ian about the news.

✗ I said to Ian about the news.

✓ He said that he was amazed.

✗ He told that he was amazed.

Tick (✓) the sentences that can use both *say* and *tell*. Rewrite them using the other verb. Add any other words if necessary. Put a cross (✗) if the sentence can't use both.

1 We didn't tell Jess anything about the party.

We didn't say anything about the party to Jess.

2 I don't think politicians ever tell the truth.

_____

3 The teacher told John that his essay was amazing.

_____

4 Charlotte said she felt the same way.

_____

5 You need to say something to them to keep them quiet.

_____

6 Please tell her to keep in touch.

_____

 **VOCABULARY**
Sharing news → SB p.94

1 ★☆☆ **Match the parts of the sentences.**

1 I'll let ☐   a you a line.
2 He broke ☐   b on the message.
3 I'll drop ☐   c in touch with me last week.
4 Give me ☐   d you know.
5 I'll pass ☐   e a call.
6 He got ☐   f the news gently.

2 ★★☆ **Complete the dialogues with the phrases in the list.**

> break the news gently | drop you a line
> give me a call | got in touch | keep in touch
> let you know | pass on the message
> retweeted

1 **A** I can't believe you're moving to Australia. That's the other side of the world.
   B Don't worry, I'll _____ . We can Skype regularly.
2 **A** I can't tell Erin about the puppy. She'll be really upset.
   B I'll tell her. And don't worry. I'll _____ .
3 **A** Leon's arriving next week, have you _____ with him yet to find out where he's staying?
   B No, not yet, I'll email him this evening.
4 **A** Wow! Your followers have _____ your comment about the book 200 times. Is that a record for you?
   B I think so.
5 **A** I've just got a message about football practice. It's been cancelled on Sunday.
   B Thanks, I'll _____ to the rest of the team.
6 **A** What time's the rehearsal on Wednesday?
   B I'm not sure. When I find out, I'll _____ .
7 **A** Right, I'm off then. I'll see you at school tomorrow.
   B Yes, _____ when you get home. And don't forget we've got an English test tomorrow.
8 **A** Well, this is goodbye then. I hope you like the new school.
   B I'll miss this place and all of you, of course. When I've settled in, I'll _____ .

> **PRONUNCIATION**
> Linking: omission of the /h/ sound
> Go to page 121. 🎧

Reporting verbs → SB p.97

3 ★★☆ **Complete the sentences with a reporting verb that means the same as the words in brackets.**

1 The actor _____ the newspaper of misquoting him. (claim)
2 The editor _____ to everybody that he had made a mistake. (tell)
3 The photographers _____ for upsetting the actor. (say sorry)
4 The politicians _____ that staying inside was the only answer. (give reasons for your opinion)
5 The sister of the famous footballer _____ selling her story to a newspaper. (be sorry about)
6 The editor was angry. He _____ her for printing the story. (complain about)
7 The council _____ to approve the building plans. (say they will)
8 The council had _____ the local residents that the building was unsafe. The boys ignored the 'Danger! Keep Out' sign on the gate. (notify)

WordWise → SB p.97
Expressions with *way*

4 ★★☆ **Complete the dialogues with the expressions in the list.**

> have it both ways | in my way | no way
> one way or another | the way | way too

1 **A** I don't want to revise. I want to go out with my friends.
   B You can't _____ . You either revise and go out after your exams or you go out and do worse in your exams.
2 **A** Have you finished that report yet?
   B Not yet. I'll get it done by 5 pm, _____ .
3 **A** Did you take that online test?
   B Yes, I think the questions were _____ easy.
4 **A** I love _____ Instagram lets you see what all your friends are up to.
   B Yes, so do I.
5 **A** Have you heard about Sarah? She's won a place on a journalism course.
   B _____ ! I can't believe it. That's brilliant.
   A I know. She really deserves it. She's worked so hard.
6 **A** Hey, Leo. Move over a bit. You're _____ . I'm trying to watch a film.
   B Sorry, I didn't realise.

REFERENCE

let you know   pass on the message

give someone a call

Sharing news

get in touch

drop someone a line

retweet   break the news   keep in touch

REPORTING VERBS

admit   regret   accuse   criticise   argue

apologise   warn   deny   agree

the way   in (my) way

have it both ways   **Expressions with way**   one way or another

no way   way too

VOCABULARY EXTRA

1 **Match the words with the definitions.**

boast | fear | guarantee
insist | reveal

1 make certain that something will happen _____

2 make known something that was surprising or secret _____

3 to speak too proudly or happily about what you have done or what you own _____

4 to say something firmly especially when others disagree or oppose what you say _____

5 worried or frightened that something bad might happen _____

2 **Complete the sentences from news articles with the correct form of reporting verbs from Exercise 1.**

1 The government _____ that they are not changing their policy.

2 All airlines _____ that they will refund the cost of all flights.

3 Police _____ that there will be problems at this weekend's music festival.

4 The thief _____ that police would never catch him.

5 The journalist _____ that he had listened to several phone conversations without permission.

3 **Complete the sentences with your own ideas.**

1 My best friend boasted that

_____

2 I fear that

_____

3 My parents insist that

_____

4 I think scientists will reveal that

_____

5 We cannot guarantee that

_____

93

A GREAT JOURNALIST

Elizabeth Cochrane was born in Pennsylvania, in the US, in 1864. She wanted to be a teacher, but at the age of 15 she had to drop out of school after a term because she and her family did not have enough money and she had to help support them.

When she was 16 years old, she read an article in a local newspaper. It said that women were not important except for having children and staying at home. She was so angry after reading it that she wrote a short letter to the editor in which she criticised the newspaper's negative representation of women. The newspaper editor was so impressed with her writing and her passion that he not only printed her letter and their response, but he agreed to offer her a job. As a writer for the newspaper, she used the name Nellie Bly. Although she was a popular writer, she was often asked to write pieces specifically aimed at what the editor thought women were interested in, for example flower shows, children and things to do with the home. Nellie, however, wanted to write more serious articles about both men and women and she began looking for a new job at a newspaper that would allow her to write more serious pieces.

In 1886, she moved to New York City, but because she was a woman, she found it very difficult to find work. Eventually, she got a job with a newspaper called *New York World*. One of her first jobs was to go inside a home for mentally ill women to report on the conditions. When she was inside, she was going to be on her own for ten days. Nellie thought it might be scary and dangerous because she suspected women in these kinds of homes were treated horribly, but she accepted the job.

Once inside the home, Nellie found that the conditions were terrible. Patients ate rotten food and drank dirty water. The hospital was dirty and there were rats everywhere. The women couldn't talk to each other, read or do anything. Often, they sat in silence for hours.

Nellie was allowed to leave after ten days after lawyers arranged her release. She wrote about her experiences. The *New York World* published her articles and as a result, she helped to improve conditions for the women in the home. She soon became one of the most famous journalists in the US and her approach to news stories soon became what we now refer to as investigative journalism.

In 1888, her investigative journalism led her to race around the world to beat the time of Phileas Fogg in the novel *Around the World in 80 Days*. She completed the journey in 72 days! Her independent spirit and natural curiosity continued and she continued to fight for women's rights all through her life until she died in 1922.

📖 READING

1 **Read the article quickly. Write down a key event for each year.**

1864   1888   1886   1922

_____   _____   _____   _____

2 **Read the article again. Mark the sentences True (T), False (F) or Doesn't Say (DS).**

1 Elizabeth Cochrane had always wanted to be a journalist. ☐

2 She wrote to the editor of a local newspaper because she did not agree with an article they had published. ☐

3 Her family were not happy about her starting work as a journalist. ☐

4 She didn't like writing stories only meant for women. ☐

5 She wasn't worried or frightened about going into the home for mentally ill women. ☐

6 She made good friends with a lot of women in the home. ☐

7 Nellie's stories of her experience helped to improve conditions for the women. ☐

8 She died while she was racing around the world. ☐

3 **CRITICAL THINKING Which statements do you think Nellie Bly would agree with? Give reasons.**

1 'You can't get anywhere in life without a good education.'

2 'Women deserve the same rights as men and they should be paid the same.'

3 'Journalists should use their heads when they write, not their hearts.'

4 'I've always had the feeling that nothing is impossible. If you want to do it, you can.'

4 **Think of a post or tweet you have seen or read recently that you disagree with. Write a comment to express your views.**

DEVELOPING *Writing*

An article for the school website

1 **INPUT** **Read Kate's article and answer the questions.**

1 What is the article about?

_____

2 What did Kate do?

_____

3 How does Kate describe her experience?

_____

STUDENT NEWS

About   Latest news   Message board   🔍

1 Last term, Kate Watkins, one of our Year 11 students, won a competition to spend a day as a news reporter with our local newspaper, the *Greendale Mail*. We asked her to tell us about her day.

2 When I arrived at the news studio, the first thing I noticed was the noise. Everyone was talking, mobiles were ringing and there were people everywhere. I was working with a journalist called Lucy. She said she had a story for me to work on, so she took me to a quiet room and she explained the background.

3 She told me that we were going to interview a young footballer who a lot of people were talking about as a future world cup star. Before we left the offices, we made a list of questions we wanted to ask. We agreed that Lucy would ask all the questions and I would take notes on her laptop. The interview went really well, but I couldn't type very fast and I apologised for making mistakes. After the interview, it was my responsibility to type up the story and Lucy checked it. Once we had agreed on the final copy, I sent it to the editor to be published.

4 In the end, my story appeared in the newspaper the next day. It was an unforgettable experience and it has made me more determined to become a journalist one day.

---

2 **ANALYSE** **Match the headings (a–d) with the paragraphs (1–4).**

a Background information ☐

b Conclusion ☐

c Introduction ☐

d Main body ☐

3 **In which paragraphs does the following information appear?**

a what the article will be about ☐

b extra details and information to set the scene ☐

c more details and an explanation of what happens, the main event(s) ☐

d the article is summed up in a few words ☐

4 **PLAN** **Imagine you have spent a week doing work experience in a workplace. Make notes on these things.**

• Preparation before the work experience started.

• Questions you want to ask.

• What happened during the work experience.

• What happened afterwards and what your dream or ambition is now.

5 **PRODUCE** **Write an article for your school website about your work experience (200–250 words). Use your notes in Exercise 4. Write your own checklist.**

✓ CHECKLIST

☐ _____

☐ _____

☐ _____

☐ _____

 **LISTENING**

1   🔊 10.02   **Read the sentences. Then listen and tick (✓) the correct option.**

The news story for the school magazine will be about …

1   the civil war in Sierra Leone. ☐

2   an orphan from Sierra Leone who became a star ballerina. ☐

3   a woman who opened an orphanage in Sierra Leone. ☐

2   🔊 10.02   **Listen again and mark the sentences T (true) or F (false).**

1   Marcus says that he doesn't want to have a story about ballet in the school magazine. ☐

2   Sarah agrees with Marcus that ballet isn't a good subject for the school magazine. ☐

3   Tom says that he likes ballet. ☐

4   Tom tells Marcus that Michaela DePrince's father had been killed in a civil war in Sierra Leone. ☐

5   After Michaela had been adopted by an American couple, she attended a ballet school. ☐

6   Michaela says that she will open a school and teach art with the money she earns from her book. ☐

DIALOGUE

1   **Complete the dialogue with the phrases in the list.**

> have you heard | have you heard about
> did you know | guess what
> you'll never believe

Jamie   ¹_____ ? Somebody stole Leo's bike yesterday.

Marie   No way! That's awful. It was a new bike as well. He got it for his birthday. I must tell Luna. Here she comes now! Luna, ²_____ Leo's bike?

Luna   Yes, his bike was stolen. But, ³_____ .

Marie   What?

Luna   The thief has brought the bike back. He left it at the school gates this morning and he left a note on the bike. ⁴_____ what it said.

Jamie   Come on then. Tell us.

Luna   It said, 'Thanks for lending me the bike. My son didn't like it so I've brought it back.' Can you believe it?

Marie   You're joking! Well at least Leo got his bike back.

Jamie   Yes, that's good news. But ⁵_____ that five bikes were stolen from the school grounds last year? And none of them were brought back. Leo's lucky.

PHRASES FOR FLUENCY → SB p.98

1   **Match the parts of the sentences.**

1   It will cost us £10, ☐

2   It's OK. <u>Don't</u> ☐

3   Karen, where ☐

4   I need some fresh air. Let's go for a walk ☐

5   <u>In any</u> ☐

6   Stop asking me. <u>It's none of</u> ☐

a   <u>on earth</u> have you been?

b   <u>your business</u>.

c   <u>or something</u>.

d   <u>at least</u>.

e   <u>bother</u> sending me a reply.

f   <u>case</u>, you know it's dangerous.

2   **Complete the dialogues with the underlined phrases in Exercise 1.**

1   **Lucia**   Would you like to write an article about Twitter for the school magazine?

Mia   It sounds interesting. I'd like to do it. But do you need me to write it right away? I'm really busy now. I don't know how _____ I'd fit it in.

Lucia   No, it's OK. You can write it next week. We won't print the magazine until the end of the month. _____ , you're the best person to write it.

2   **Tim**   Did Jeremy tell you what happened?

Luke   No, he didn't. I asked him but he said _____ .

3   **Matt**   Let's ask Nick to come to the park with us _____ .

Chris   Good idea. We can take our bikes.

4   **Naomi**   My mum said that Claude Monet had painted over 1,000 paintings and there would be _____ 500 paintings on display at the exhibition.

Emily   Well, it sounds like you're going to be very busy looking at paintings so _____ sending me any texts or emails or anything. You can tell me all about it when you get back.

B2 First for Schools

EXAM GUIDE:

In Part 1 of the B2 First for Schools Reading and Use of English exam, you will read a short text. This text has eight gaps for you to complete. For each gap, you have to choose one of four options. This part of the exam tests your vocabulary knowledge, including phrasal verbs and collocations or idioms. The options often include words with similar meanings. However, you may also have to rely on your knowledge of grammar to choose the correct options.

- Before you try to fill in the gaps, read the text quickly to get a general idea of what it is about.
- Then, for each gap, re-read the whole sentence and pay close attention to the words just before and after the gap. These words will be the most important to help you choose the correct answer.
- Eliminate any options you are sure are wrong and focus your attention on the others.
- For phrasal verbs, one of the words will be given, and you will have to choose the other one.

1 **For questions 1–8, read the text below and decide which answer (A, B, C, or D) best fits each gap. There is an example at the beginning (0).**

Example:

0   A lately   B shortly   C currently ✔   D immediately

The world's first daily newspaper

The internet is **(0) ...** changing how people consume their daily news. For over 300 years, however, the principal means of **(1) ...** up with national and world events was through printed daily newspapers.

The first ever printed daily newspaper, the *Daily Courant*, was published in London on 11 March 1702. It was written by a woman called Elizabeth Mallet. At that time, women were generally **(2) ...** educated and were expected to look after the children and the home rather than taking **(3) ...** employment. Knowing that readers would be unlikely to take a newspaper **(4) ...** if they discovered it had been created by a woman, Mallet felt **(5) ...** into using a man's name on the *Daily Courant* rather than her own.

(6) ... modern multi-page printed newspapers, *The Daily Courant* appeared on just a single sheet. On one side, there were **(7) ...** Mallet had written of news stories from around the world. On the other, there were adverts. Mallet **(8) ...** only to provide the facts, thus allowing readers to make up their own minds about the story.

1 A getting	B setting	C holding	D keeping
2 A poorly	B weakly	C awfully	D thinly
3 A rewarded	B paid	C waged	D monied
4 A seriously	B honestly	C sincerely	D openly
5 A obliged	B required	C forced	D pressed
6 A Moreover	B Despite	C Except	D Unlike
7 A conclusions	B summaries	C judgements	D considerations
8 A claimed	B argued	C stated	D emphasised

CONSOLIDATION

🎧 LISTENING

1 🔊 10.03 **Listen to the news item. Tick (✓) the three things that are talked about.**

1. Someone who is looking for a job. ☐
2. Someone who has left their job. ☐
3. Someone who might lose their job. ☐
4. Someone who appeared in a magazine. ☐
5. Someone who has won a prize. ☐

2 🔊 10.03 **Listen again. Complete the missing information in each sentence with no more than five words.**

1. Mr Godber said he
   _____
   about the time he worked for the club.
2. Mr Godber thinks some things
   _____ way.
3. Mr Godber wants to
   _____
   his future.
4. Ms Green has _____
   for sending the Tweet.
5. The college director thinks the Tweet had
   _____
   of the college.
6. It's possible that the college
   _____
   Ms Green's contract.
7. Annabel Lee won her prize by
   _____ .
8. Annabel will be going
   _____ a week.

Ⓖ GRAMMAR

3 **Circle the correct options.**

1. My brother asked me *to help / would I help* him.
2. I wish it *isn't / wasn't* raining.
3. I think it's time we *get / got* in touch with them again.
4. I asked him *if he wanted / did he want* to read the book.
5. If only you *told / had told* me yesterday, then I could have done something about it.
6. I'm sure he wishes now that he *didn't buy / hadn't bought* that cheap tablet.
7. He asked me why *had I left / I had left* the cinema in the middle of the film.
8. I really would prefer it if you *didn't / don't* put olives on the pizza.
9. Take any flavour you want, but I'd sooner you *leave / left* the vanilla one for me.

🅰 VOCABULARY

4 **Match the parts of the sentences.**

1. He apologised ☐
2. I've always regretted ☐
3. They're on holiday but they dropped ☐
4. My parents warned me ☐
5. Try not to dwell ☐
6. He's been accused ☐
7. You promised to do it but you really let ☐
8. As soon as I find out, I'll let ☐
9. I wanted to go, but other things got ☐
10. My attempts to be nice to him didn't work ☐

a. on things that happened in the past.
b. me down.
c. for being late.
d. you know.
e. me a line yesterday.
f. not learning to play a musical instrument.
g. not to make too much noise.
h. of taking money that wasn't his.
i. in my way.
j. out very well.

5 **Complete the missing words.**

1. It was really a matter of luck – things just didn't go my w_____ .
2. I didn't do it! I d_____ it completely!
3. Well it wasn't her fault so you can't b_____ her for what happened.
4. She lives in Canada now, so we keep in t_____ by email and social media.
5. She's finished university – she got her d_____ last month.
6. It doesn't matter that you didn't win. Things don't always work out the w_____ we want them.
7. I'm going to the factory twice a week to get some work e_____ .
8. The maths exam was quite hard. Some of the questions were really t_____ .
9. It's bad news and I don't know how to b_____ it to him.
10. She's highly qualified – she's a g_____ of a top university.

DIALOGUE

6 Complete the dialogue with the phrases in the list. There are two you don't need.

> at least | don't bother | I'd rather
> on earth | in any case | none of her business
> I'd prefer it | never guess

Max You'll ¹_____ what I heard.

Millie What?

Max Jack South had a huge argument with his parents and they've grounded him. He isn't allowed to go out with his friends for ²_____ two weeks!

Millie Well, Max, ³_____ you didn't tell me things like that. I'm not very interested. And ⁴_____ , it might not be true.

Max Well, I wasn't sure it was true, until Sophie Payne told me and she's never wrong about these things.

Millie Well, it's ⁵_____ . Nor yours, either, to be honest.

Max Well I'm sorry, I didn't think you'd be so upset. It's just a bit of news, that's all.

Millie Sorry, Max, but it's gossip. If you hear more gossip like that, please ⁶_____ telling me, OK?

Max OK, Millie. Well, it was nice to see you anyway – I think.

7 Read the article and answer the questions.

1 How is meditation believed to have started?
_____

2 When did it start to become adopted in the West?
_____

3 How is meditation usually done?
_____

4 How do you need to walk while meditating?
_____

5 What do you need to concentrate on while walking?
_____

6 Where is the best place to do walking meditation?
_____

7 When should you not do walking meditation?
_____

8 What are the benefits of practising?
_____

Ways to relax –
Walking meditation

A lot of people around the world practise meditation – a technique for becoming very calm and relaxed. It's most commonly practised by essentially concentrating on only one thing and cutting out the outside world. There isn't a lot of recorded history about meditation, but we know that it started a long, long time ago. It's believed that meditation may have been discovered as long ago as the days of primitive people who hunted for wild animals, who, when cooking the meat over fires, began to stare at the flames and think in a different, more relaxed way. There are Indian writings mentioning meditation that are around 5,000 years old!

Thousands of years after meditation took off in the East, it began to be adopted in Western cultures, too, becoming popular mostly around the middle of the 20th century. Researchers also began looking at the effects of meditation and more and more was understood about the many benefits it brought to its practitioners.

Now, most people think of meditation as something you normally do sitting down in a cross-legged position and with your eyes closed and very often it is. But there is another kind of meditation that has recently been made popular by the Vietnamese teacher Thich Nhat Hanh: walking meditation.

People who do walking meditation say that it helps them get into a meditative state quite easily, through concentrating on the actual act of walking. You need to walk fairly slowly and calmly, of course, but not too differently from a normal pace. And as you walk, the idea is to get your mind to think about nothing else than what you and your body are doing: walking. Each time you find you're starting to think about something else, you try to bring your mind back, to concentrate on your feet and their contact with the ground, and how your arms swing as you walk.

It can be done anywhere, even in confined spaces, but most people say it is best practised outside, in an environment with nature around, if possible. You should do it for about 20 minutes and not combine it with anything else. Don't do walking meditation while you're going to school, work or the shops. Do it as an activity for its own sake, it's much better that way. Don't think about your destination. Walking meditation is all about going, not arriving.

Sounds easy? In a way it is, although like anything else, it needs practice and the more you do it, the better you get at it and the richer the rewards. It is a way towards dealing with the stresses and strains of everyday life and towards living more peacefully. As Thich Nhat Hanh says: 'Peace is every step'.

 WRITING

8 Write a paragraph about the way(s) that you relax (100–120 words).

Grammar video
▶ 29

GRAMMAR
Speculating (past, present and future)

→ SB p.104

1 ★☆☆ **Do these sentences refer to the past, present or future? Write PA (past), PR (present) or F (future).**

1 You might have left your passport at the hotel. ☐
2 Don't touch that frog. It may be poisonous. ☐
3 United are bound to lose. ☐
4 It could be Grandma who sent you the flowers. ☐
5 Her teachers say she's likely to pass. ☐
6 She can't have left the country. She hasn't got a passport. ☐

2 ★★☆ **Circle the correct options.**

1 The cat might *take / have taken* it.

2 Wow. That must *be / have been* exciting.

3 He can't *go / have gone* far. He isn't wearing any boots.

4 The people at the information office must *know / have known* a good hotel.

5 Take lots of water. You're *bound to / could* get thirsty.

6 Come on. The man on the radio said the roads *are likely to / must* get really busy today.

3 ★★★ **Complete the second sentence so that it means the same as the first sentence using between two and five words. Use the word in capital letters. Do not change the form of this word.**

1 There'll be rain for sure this weekend. We're planning a picnic. **BOUND TO**
_____ this weekend. We're planning a picnic.

2 They're speaking Portuguese so there's a chance they're Brazilian. **COULD**
They _____
Brazilian because they're speaking Portuguese.

3 Toby got top marks in the test. I'm sure he spent all week studying for it. **MUST**
Toby _____
studying to get top marks in the test.

4 Police believe there's a possibility one of the robbers worked at the bank in the past. **MIGHT**
Police believe one of the robbers _____ at the bank in the past.

5 I don't think anyone will beat last year's winner at Wimbledon this year. **CERTAIN**
I think last year's winner _____ at Wimbledon this year.

6 The cat must be outside. I can't find it. **CAN'T BE**
The cat _____ .
I can't find it.

7 Scientists think the population of our planet will probably pass 8 billion by 2030. **LIKELY**
Scientists think the population of our planet _____ 8 billion by 2030.

PRONUNCIATION
Stress on modal verbs for speculation
Go to page 121.

SHOOT FOR THE STARS | UNIT 11

Cause and effect linkers → SB p.107

4 ★☆☆ **Match the parts of the sentences.**

1 The football match was cancelled ☐
2 As a result of her hard work, ☐
3 His parents took away his computer ☐
4 She isn't very popular. ☐
5 Due to the high price, ☐
6 She got a record contract ☐
7 Because of his high temperature, ☐
8 He's quite short for his age. ☐

a because of his bad school report.
b Consequently not many people came to her party.
c as a result of her popularity on YouTube.
d his mother didn't let him go to school.
e due to crowd trouble.
f Consequently lots of people think he's younger than he is.
g not many children went on the school skiing trip.
h she raised £1,000 for charity.

5 ★★☆ **Complete the second sentence so that it means the same as the first.**

I'm sorry I was late to school today.

1 My alarm clock was broken. I overslept.
As a result of _____.
2 My room's a mess. I couldn't find my trainers.
Due to _____.
3 My bike's got a flat tyre. I couldn't ride it to school.
Because of _____.
4 I've got a twisted ankle. I couldn't run to the bus stop.
_____ as a result of
_____.
5 There was an accident. The bus journey was really slow.
_____ due to
_____.
6 I arrived at 9.30. The school gate was locked.
I couldn't get into school because of _____.

6 ★★★ **Think of three different ways to finish each of these sentences.**

1 The launch of the rocket was delayed
due to _____
because of _____
as a result of _____
2 Alan didn't get to be an astronaut
due to _____
because of _____
as a result of _____
3 The astronaut had to return early from the space station
due to _____
because of _____
as a result of _____
4 The school trip to the space centre was cancelled
due to _____
because of _____
as a result of _____

GET IT RIGHT!

Modals of speculation

Learners often make mistakes when using modals of speculation, either using the wrong modal or the wrong tense.

✓ You **can't** have been very happy when you heard the news!

✗ You *mustn't* have been very happy when you heard the news!

✓ You should **have helped** her to finish her project. She didn't finish it on time.

✗ You should *help* her to finish her project. She didn't finish it on time.

Circle the correct options.

1 A Lidia got top marks in her exams!
  B She *must / may* be over the moon.
2 George's been to London once before. He *might / can't* know the best things to see.
3 You *can't / mustn't* be serious! I'm not doing that.
4 I might *have seen / see* the film, but I can't remember.
5 The film was amazing. No one could have *directed / direct* it better than him.
6 We *must / might* be very early. There's no one else here!

VOCABULARY
Space idioms

→ SB p.105

1 ⭐☆☆ **Match the sentences.**

1 His costume was out of this world. ☐
2 Come on. It isn't rocket science. ☐
3 Her fans are always starry-eyed. ☐
4 He's very down to earth really. ☐
5 They're over the moon. ☐
6 We go to the beach once in a blue moon. ☐

a They love absolutely everything she does.
b They've just won first prize in a writing competition.
c We hardly ever do it.
d It was really amazing.
e He's very normal and unpretentious.
f I know you can work it out.

2 ⭐⭐☆ **Match the pictures with the sentences in Exercise 1.**

 A
 B
 C
 D
 E
 F

Adjectives commonly used to describe film

→ SB p.107

3 ⭐☆☆ **Find eight adjectives commonly used to describe films.**

G	M	O	V	I	N	G	T	F	U	L	E	A
N	S	P	Q	O	W	I	E	U	R	Y	J	C
I	Y	T	A	L	S	K	D	J	F	H	G	T
K	Z	M	U	X	N	C	B	V	R	G	R	I
A	L	A	T	N	E	M	I	T	N	E	S	O
T	Q	Z	A	W	N	X	S	I	E	C	R	N
H	V	F	T	B	G	I	L	Y	N	H	U	P
T	M	J	I	K	L	L	N	I	O	P	T	A
A	L	A	B	Y	I	K	S	G	E	I	S	C
E	L	B	A	R	O	M	E	M	A	E	L	K
R	U	E	H	A	C	R	A	C	S	O	G	E
B	U	T	F	A	R	F	E	T	C	H	E	D

4 ⭐⭐☆ **Circle the option which is NOT possible.**

1 The view from the top of the mountain was absolutely …
   a stunning   b far-fetched   c breathtaking
2 I didn't expect the end of the film to be so … I cried.
   a moving   b sentimental   c action-packed
3 It was a really … game of football – the best I've seen for ages.
   a action-packed   b thrilling   c sentimental
4 The play was quite … but I still enjoyed it.
   a sentimental   b memorable   c far-fetched
5 That high-speed car chase in the film was absolutely …!
   a action-packed   b thrilling   c moving
6 They looked … on their prom night.
   a memorable   b stunning   c breathtaking

5 ⭐⭐☆ **Write the name of a film that is …**

1 stunning
_____
2 a bit far-fetched
_____
3 breath-taking
_____
4 thrilling
_____
5 too sentimental
_____
6 action-packed from beginning to end
_____
7 memorable
_____
8 moving
_____

REFERENCE

Space idioms

- out of this world
- rocket science
- down to earth
- once in a blue moon
- over the moon
- starry-eyed

Adjectives commonly used to describe films

- breath-taking
- memorable
- thrilling
- sentimental
- moving
- action-packed
- far-fetched
- stunning

VOCABULARY EXTRA

1 **Read the definitions and match them with the correct words in the list.**

> constellation | galaxy
> meteor shower
> satellite | solar system

1 the sun and group of planets that move around it: _____

2 any of the groups of stars in the sky which form a pattern when seen from Earth and each group has its own name: _____

3 one of the independent groups of stars in the universe: _____

4 an occasion when a number of meteors move fast across the sky at night: _____

5 a device in space that travels round the earth to collect information or communicate by radio, TV, etc. or a natural object moving around a larger object in space: _____

2 **Choose the correct options.**

The earth is one of nine planets which orbits the Sun in our [1]*meteor shower / solar system*, but there are also almost 5000 [2]*satellites / constellations* orbiting the earth. Groups of stars all have their own [3]*solar system / galaxy*. However, finding a(n) [4]*constellation / orbit* in the sky can be difficult and a star map is useful. When you are looking for stars, you might see a [5]*meteor shower / constellation* moving quickly across the sky. They are sometimes called shooting stars.

3 **Complete the space facts with the correct word. Then choose the correct answer.**

SPACE QUIZ

❶ The largest planet in the _____ is …
   a Mars   b Venus   c Jupiter

❷ The Milky Way _____ contains about … stars.
   a 100 billion   b 500,000   c 1 million

❸ The Moon is the Earth's only natural _____ . It orbits the Earth every …
   a 7 days   b 20 days   c 27.3 days

❹ A _____ called the Geminids from the _____ of Gemini usually occurs in mid … every year.
   a October   b December   c November

Answers
1 solar system C   2 galaxy A   3 satellite C
4 meteor shower; constellation B

103

A DAY ON THE
INTERNATIONAL SPACE STATION

What is it like for the international crew living and working on the ISS when mission control turns on the lights for them each day at 6 am?

A _____

They get up, but they don't have a shower because that can be difficult due to zero gravity – everything floats in space, including water. Astronauts use some liquid soap with a little water and a special shampoo without water to wash their hair. Any water they use is certain to be recycled.

B _____

The first meal of the day is breakfast, but their food is dried and it can't be eaten unless water is added. Ketchup and mustard are available, but because of zero gravity, the astronauts can't use normal salt and pepper. They must be in a liquid form. If they weren't liquids, the astronauts might end up with salt or pepper in their eyes, or the powder could cause problems inside the ISS or damage the equipment.

C _____

The ISS is a floating science research lab and the astronauts do research and experiments. One of the most important aims of the ISS is for doctors to see what effect zero-gravity has on the human body and how it can adjust to living in space for long periods of time. The astronauts check the space equipment regularly to make sure it is working properly and they must update the computer equipment, too. Mission Control on Earth communicates with the ISS regularly and sends voice messages or emails with instructions for the crew.

D _____

This is a very important part of the astronauts' daily routine because they must prevent bone and muscle loss. They exercise for two hours a day. As a result of zero gravity, exercise equipment like weights, exercise bikes and running machines have to be specially designed for space.

E _____

After a long, hard day at work on the space station, the astronauts go to bed at the same time each night. However, there are quite a few differences. There is no 'up' or 'down' in space, so astronauts have to sleep in special sleeping bags in their own cabins and attach themselves to something so they don't float around and bump into things during the night. They can sleep in any position so some of them choose to sleep standing up. They try to sleep for eight hours a night.

F _____

Everyone needs to have free time and a bit of fun, so when the astronauts are orbiting Earth they take a break now and again. The most popular free-time activity is looking out of the window. It doesn't sound very exciting, but in space the astronauts love watching the Earth spin below them and taking photos. They also enjoy watching sunsets or sunrises every 45 minutes. They don't have to work at the weekend, so they watch films, play music, read books, play card games and talk to their families. Some astronauts even play the guitar in space and make music videos.

READING

1 Read the article quickly. Match the titles with the paragraphs. There are two titles you do not need.

1 A good night's sleep
2 Research
3 Free time
4 Work
5 Engineering
6 Exercise
7 Personal hygiene
8 Food

2 Read the article again and answer the questions.

1 Why is washing a problem in space and what do the ISS astronauts do?

_____

2 What is the problem with salt and pepper in space?

_____

3 Why are doctors interested in what life is like for the astronauts?

_____

4 How is exercise different in space?

_____

5 How do astronauts stop themselves floating away during the night?

_____

6 What is one of the astronauts favourite free-time activities?

_____

3 CRITICAL THINKING Astronauts spend a lot of time with the same people. What advice would you give someone who was going to spend a lot of time on their own or with the same people for a long period of time? Think about these things.

- the best ways to deal with the isolation
- work–life balance
- getting away from each other
- getting away from work

4 Imagine spending a day on the ISS. Write a blog post about what it's like (80–100 words).

DEVELOPING *Writing*

A film review

1 INPUT **Read the review. Who are these characters?**

1 Ayesha

_____

2 Quill, Gamora, Drax, Rocket, Groot

_____

3 Nebula

_____

4 Ego

_____

Guardians of the Galaxy Vol. 2 (2017) ★★★★★★★★★★

1 This sci-fi action film features the vocal talents of Vin Diesel and Bradley Cooper as well as the actors Zoe Saldana, Chris Pratt and Dave Bautista.

2 The leader of the Sovereign race, Ayesha, asks the Guardians of the Galaxy to destroy a monster to protect her valuable batteries. Quill, Gamora, Drax, Rocket and Groot defeat the monster and Ayesha allows Gamora's adopted sister Nebula to return to the Guardians. However, Rocket steals some of the batteries and the Sovereign people attack the Guardian's spacecraft. That is until a mysterious ship destroys the Sovereign fleet and the Guardians crash on a planet. While they are there, the Guardians learn that the ship that helped them is owned by Ego. He claims to be Quill's father and invites Quill to visit his planet. Who is Ego and what will happen on his planet? Will Peter Quill find out about his family? Can the Guardians defend the galaxy again?

3 *Guardians of the Galaxy* has plenty in it to appeal to everyone over the age of 12 and it is an enjoyable way to spend two hours. Although the story is a little far-fetched, it is action-packed with lots of hilarious moments. The soundtrack is memorable and my favourite song is definitely *Mr Blue Sky*.

4 To sum up, I would rate this film nine out of ten. I'd recommend watching it online if you didn't see it the first time around.

2 ANALYSE **In which paragraph of the review can you find the following?**

a a brief summary of the action or the story ☐
b a recommendation ☐
c the type of film and the actors ☐
d what the writer liked or didn't like ☐

3 Read the review again and answer the questions.

1 What background information does the writer give in the first paragraph?

_____

2 Write a summary of the story in two sentences.

_____

_____

3 What did the writer like (or not like) about the film?

_____

4 What recommendation does the writer make?

_____

4 PLAN **Choose a film, play or book to review. Make notes for each paragraph.**

• background details
• a summary of the action
• your opinion and reasons
• your recommendation

5 PRODUCE **Write your review (200–250 words). Use your notes in Exercise 4. Write your own checklist.**

✓ CHECKLIST

☐ _____

☐ _____

☐ _____

☐ _____

 **LISTENING**

1 🔊 **11.02** **Listen to Matt giving a presentation to his class. The title of his talk is: 'Should we be doing more to explore space?' Tick (✓) the two reasons Matt gives in support of space exploration.**

1 We might find gases and minerals that aren't on Earth and that could help us. ☐

2 We could develop places in space for people to live. ☐

3 We might find substances that could help us with medical problems. ☐

4 We could find ways to grow food for people on Earth. ☐

2 🔊 **11.02** **Listen again and answer the questions.**

1 Why is Matt giving the talk today?

_____

2 What does Matt think is one of the biggest problems on Earth?

_____

3 What does he think would be the consequence of not doing anything about it?

_____

4 Why does Jake disagree with Matt?

_____

5 What does Hazel say is 'never going to happen'?

_____

6 What does Nora say about money?

_____

7 What does Matt say might have influenced his ideas too much?

_____

8 How does the class generally react to Matt's talk?

_____

3 **Write a short paragraph to say what you think about Matt's ideas.**

DIALOGUE

1 **Complete the dialogue with the missing lines (a–g). There are two lines you do not need.**

Jamie   What's up, Lina?

Lina   Nothing really. I'm just having a really bad day.

Jamie   ¹_____

Lina   Well, first of all I missed the school bus, so I had to walk to school.

Jamie   ²_____

Lina   Of course I was. Miss Stevens wasn't very happy and her mood didn't get any better when I told her I'd left my homework at home. It was a Geography project that I'd spent days on. She said I'm going to lose five marks just because it's late.

Jamie   ³_____

Lina   That's what I told her and that's when she decided that I was being rude and that's why I had to spend break and lunchtime in the classroom on my own.

Jamie   ⁴_____

Lina   Yes, which was really bad because Mr Wilson was holding auditions for the school orchestra at lunchtime and I couldn't go.

Jamie   ⁵_____

Lina   I hope so, but knowing my luck today he won't.

a   What a shame, but I'm sure he will give you another chance.

b   Oh dear. Better luck next time.

c   Poor you. Were you late?

d   Oh no. So you missed both break times?

e   How terrible. Why don't you try again?

f   Oh dear. So what's happened?

g   How terrible. That doesn't seem very fair.

2 **Choose one of these first lines and use it to write a short dialogue (8–10 lines).**

• My dad says I can't go to Rob's party on Saturday.

• I lost my wallet when I was shopping yesterday.

• Have you heard? Sally's broken her leg.

_____
_____
_____
_____
_____
_____
_____
_____
_____
_____

B2 First for Schools

EXAM GUIDE

In Part 3 of the First for Schools Reading and Use of English Exam, you will have to complete a short text that has eight gaps. This part of the exam tests your knowledge of vocabulary, grammar and spelling. You will be given a 'base word' at the end of each line with a gap, which you will have to transform so that it fits into the sentence.

- Before you start, read the whole text to get a general understanding of what it is about.
- Remember to use the word at the end of the line of each gap, and not any other words.
- You have to 'transform' the base word in some way. This means you have to turn it into a noun, adjective or adverb of the same word family. You might have to add a negative prefix, and/or change the word type by adding a suffix.
- Once you have transformed the base word, re-read the whole sentence to make sure it makes sense.
- You must spell each word correctly to get points, so double check.
- If your answer is a noun, remember to check whether it should be plural or singular.

1   **For questions 1–8, read the text below. Use the word given in capitals at the end of some of the lines to form a word that fits in the gap in the same line. There is an example at the beginning (0).**

Example: **0** *SOUTHERN*

Lake Baikal

Lake Baikal is a huge lake located in the **(0)** _____*southern*_____ part of Russia. It is 636 km long and has an average **(1)** _____ of around 50 km. Lake Baikal is **(2)** _____ deep, reaching down to a maximum of 1,642 metres, making it the deepest lake in the world. It holds more water than all of the Great Lakes in North America **(3)** _____ .

The climate close to Lake Baikal is **(4)** _____ milder than that of the surrounding region. Despite this, the surface of the lake freezes in early January and doesn't melt completely until May. Although this is **(5)** _____ for anyone who normally travels by boat, the ice is **(6)** _____ enough to allow vehicles to be driven over it for at least part of the winter.

In summer, water temperature rises to between 10°C and 12°C. The water in Lake Baikal is incredibly clear. Anyone **(7)** _____ enough to dive in the lake will find that objects remain **(8)** _____ underwater even at distances of 40 metres and above.

SOUTH
WIDE
ASTONISH

COMBINATION
CONSIDER

CONVENIENT
SUBSTANCE

ADVENTURE
VISION

Grammar video

GRAMMAR

Passive report structures → SB p.112

1 ★★☆ **Complete the sentences with a passive report structure of the words in brackets. Then match the sentences to the pictures.**

1 The climbers _____ to be halfway up the mountain. (believe)

2 The space probe _____ to arrive on Mars in six years' time. (expect)

3 The last dodo on Earth _____ to have died in 1662. (say)

4 The jug in the museum _____ to be more than a thousand years old. (think)

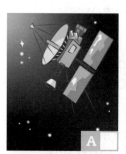 

2 ★★☆ **Complete the texts using a word from list A and then a phrase from list B.**

A [is | are | is | are]   B [to have given | to be   to have made | to have]

Gávea Rock

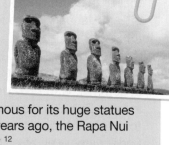

The Gávea Rock is a mountain in the Tijuca Forest in Rio de Janeiro, Brazil. Portuguese explorers
¹_____ thought
²_____ it its
name in the 1500s. The Ancient Phoenicians ³_____ said ⁴_____ a face in the rock in the shape of their emperor's face although archaeologists are not sure if this is true. May to September
⁵_____ known ⁶_____ the best time to climb the rock because although it is winter, it isn't very cold. At 844 metres high, it's a difficult climb but it's worth it – it ⁷_____ said ⁸_____ the most amazing views of Rio!

A [is | are | were | are]   B [to have | to look after   to have arrived | to be]

Rapa Nui

Rapa Nui, or Easter Island, is more than 3,500 kilometres off the coast of Chile. It ⁹_____ thought ¹⁰_____ one of the world's most isolated but inhabited islands. The island is famous for its huge statues of heads called *moai*. More than 900 years ago, the Rapa Nui people ¹¹_____ thought ¹²_____ on the island and created the statues. It is believed that each statue took a year to complete. Most of the statues face towards the villages on the island and ¹³_____ said ¹⁴_____ the inhabitants. Some of the statues ¹⁵_____ known ¹⁶_____ connections to food production and water.

3 ★★★ **Write sentences using passive report structures that are true for you.**

0 *London is said to be one of the most expensive cities in the world.*

1 My home town _____

2 My house / flat _____

3 The most beautiful place in my country _____

The passive: verbs with two objects

→ SB p.115

4 ⭐☆☆ **Read these sentences. Circle the direct object and underline the indirect object.**

0 They gave (the child) <u>some medicine</u>.
1 The newsagent showed Penny the new magazine.
2 They offered the students free books.
3 Someone promised a room with a view to Kenneth.
4 The police didn't give any information to the reporters.
5 Someone sent me a strange email.
6 The university offered her a place.
7 They sold faulty goods to their customers.
8 The company gave excellent references to the students on work experience.

5 ⭐⭐☆ **Rewrite the sentences using the passive. Use the person as the subject.**

0 Someone offered me a cup of coffee.
   I was offered a cup of coffee.
1 Someone showed the photos to Jim.
   _____
2 They promised Jackie a part in the new play.
   _____
3 People ask film stars a lot of questions.
   _____
4 Someone gave Eric a new hoodie for his birthday.
   _____
5 People are going to pay the inventor a lot of money for her idea.
   _____
6 Someone sent an advertisement for sports equipment to my grandmother.
   _____
7 They offered my school a new IT centre.
   _____
8 No one told him the truth.
   _____
9 They didn't give the customers a refund.
   _____
10 The company didn't offer work experience to the students.
   _____

6 ⭐⭐⭐ **Write two complete sentences from each prompt. Put the more appropriate one first.**

0 Famous painting / give / art gallery
   The art gallery was given a famous painting.
   A famous painting was given to the art gallery
1 The new students / tell / the class rules
   _____
   _____
2 My father / offer / a job in London
   _____
   _____
3 The new film / show / a large audience
   _____
   _____
4 A trophy / present / the winner
   _____
   _____
5 Alice / send / some flowers / for her birthday
   _____
   _____

GET IT *RIGHT!*

The passive

When using the passive learners often use the wrong tense. They also sometimes use the infinitive instead of the past participle.

✓ *We're all happy now that a decision **has been taken**.*
✗ *We're all happy now that a decision is taken.*
✓ *This picture had been **taken** three years before.*
✗ *This picture had been take three years before.*

Correct the mistake in each sentence.

1 There are still many places on Earth that haven't been explore yet.
   _____
2 A research trip to the glacier is taken this week.
   _____
3 He left the room after a joke has been made about him.
   _____
4 Every effort has made to find the missing man but to no avail.
   _____
5 A lot of progress is been made recently in Sam's work.
   _____
6 It's essential for good communication to be establish between nations.
   _____

VOCABULARY
Geographical features
→ SB p.112

1 ★☆☆ **Complete the crossword.**

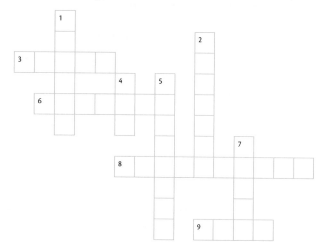

1 The Grand … in Arizona, US was carved out of the rock by the Colorado river over many thousands of years.

2 Visitors to Antarctica can see the Lambert … . It's the biggest ice formation in the world.

3 Some sand … in the Sahara Desert occasionally have snow on them.

4 About 1,000 people live in floating villages in Ha Long … , in Vietnam.

5 & 7 The Himalayas are a … in Asia.

6 In 2010 a … in Iceland erupted and caused a lot of problems for planes.

8 There are three very high … at Niagara on the border between Canada and the US.

9 There are over 1,500 different species of fish in the Great Barrier … in Australia.

Verb + noun collocations
→ SB p.115

2 ★☆☆ **Circle the correct options.**

1 It isn't nice to *make / take* fun of other people.

2 We all *made / gave* a deal to organise a party after our exams.

3 My little brother loves *playing / doing* the fool. It can be irritating sometimes.

4 Robert is very shy and finds it hard to *take / make* friends.

5 I've already *made / done* a lot of research for my project, but it isn't finished yet.

6 Lia was *taking / making* a photo when she dropped her phone.

7 The teacher told Jack's mother that he had *made / done* good progress that term.

8 Can you *make / give* me an example to help me understand it more easily?

3 ★★☆ **Complete the sentences.**

1 What would you _____ a complaint about in a restaurant?

2 What examples of bravery can you _____ ?

3 What is the longest journey you have ever _____ ?

4 What advice would you _____ to a friend who has just failed an exam?

5 If you had to _____ a speech in public, how would you feel?

6 What's the best joke you have ever _____ on someone?

4 ★★★ **Write your answers to the questions in Exercise 3.**

1 _____
2 _____
3 _____
4 _____
5 _____
6 _____

5 ★★★ **Rewrite the sentences using the words in capitals. Use the collocations on page 111 to help you.**

0 Do you hope for something on your birthday? **WISH**
   Do you make a wish on your birthday?

1 I think that I am getting better at the piano. **PROGRESS**

   _____

2 Sally tried hard to reach the top shelf. **EFFORT**

   _____

3 She said that she wasn't happy about the food. **COMPLAINT**

   _____

4 Matthew accepted Lucio's offer of a lift home. **ADVANTAGE**

   _____

5 I forgot Jo's birthday, so to compensate, I gave her some chocolates. **AMENDS**

   _____

REFERENCE

Geographical features

waterfall — bay — canyon — dune — glacier
volcano — reef — mountain range

VERB + NOUN COLLOCATIONS

do	give	make		play	take
research	advice	amends	a joke	the fool	advantage of
	an example	a complaint	a journey	a joke	advice
	a speech	a deal	a wish	a part	a decision
		a decision	money		a joke
		an effort	progress		a journey
		friends	a speech		a photo
		fun of			revenge

VOCABULARY EXTRA

1   Label the pictures with the words in the list.

coastline | cove | peak
plateau | swamp | valley

1 _____

2 _____

3 _____

4 _____

5 _____

6 _____

2   Match the words in Exercise 1 with the definitions.

1 the highest point _____

2 an area of lowland between hills or mountains, often with a river running through it _____

3 the particular shape of a coast, especially as seen from above, from the sea or on a map _____

4 a large flat area of land that is high above sea level

_____

5 a curved part of a coast that partly surrounds an area of water _____

6 an area of very wet, soft land _____

3   Complete the descriptions.

1 The Atchafalaya _____ in south central Louisiana is the biggest in the US. It is a combination of wetlands and rivers.

2 Death _____ is actually a desert in Eastern California. It is one of the hottest places in the world.

3 The highest and biggest _____ in the world is in Tibet. It is 55 million years old and is part of the Himalayan mountain range.

4 Lulworth _____ on the Jurassic coast in the south-east coast of England is a popular tourist attraction with more than 1 million visitors a year. There are 10 million-year-old fossils there.

5 The _____ of Mount Everest is 8,850 metres above sea level.

6 Canada has the longest _____ in the world. It is 202,080 kilometres long with the Pacific Ocean to the west, the Atlantic Ocean to the east and the Arctic Ocean to the north.

Hidden treasure

When we hear the word 'exploration', we tend to think of people going off into deserted parts of the world, places like caves or deserts. But for a lot of people, exploration means finding out more about the town or city where they live: urban exploration (or UE). And the idea is that, instead of exploring the natural world, people explore man-made structures in cities, especially those places that city-dwellers don't usually get to see. What kinds of places? Well, all kinds of places, but often tunnels underground, old ruined buildings, or any kind of abandoned structure. Curiosity takes the explorers there and often, they record the places by taking photos. Many urban explorers make a point of posting their photos on social media sites, and attract a large following.

Of course, unexpected things can happen. One example is from 2014 in Ontario, Canada. An urban explorer and photographer called Dave heard about a derelict house and decided to go in to take photos. He moved around the house, taking photos of the rooms and the possessions that had been left behind. Then something caught his eye. In the corner of a bed, under an old mattress, something was sticking out. When Dave investigated, it turned out to be a bag containing about $7,000 in old American and Canadian bank notes. Some of the bundles of money had handwritten notes with dates from the 1960s and 70s on them.

One of the principles of urban exploration is: 'take nothing but pictures, leave nothing but footprints'. So, Dave had some more exploring to do – to try to find the owner of the money. He did some research into the house and who had owned it. Eventually, he found the granddaughter of the last people to have lived in the house. Her grandparents had owned a fruit stall in Ontario and kept their money under a mattress – and somehow, it had been forgotten. Dave gave the money to the woman, who was so grateful she cried.

Urban exploration can be a dangerous business – going into ruined buildings, or old tunnels, brings risks and there have been instances of explorers being killed by, for example, falling off a roof. It is also sometimes illegal – in their search for places where people never go and where they can take photos from brand new angles, urban explorers often end up going into places where they are not allowed. Urban exploration can uncover hidden treasure and bring joy, but it's important to remember the risks.

📖 READING

1 Look at the photos and the title of the blog. Tick (✓) what you think the blog is about. Then read the article to check.

1 Someone hid some money in an old building. ☐
2 Someone paid a lot of money for an old house. ☐
3 Someone found money in an old house. ☐
4 Someone found treasure while building a house. ☐

2 Read the blog again and answer the questions.

1 What examples are given of places that urban explorers go to?

_____

2 Why did Dave go into the house?

_____

3 Why did Dave decide not to keep the money?

_____

4 Where had the money come from?

_____

5 Why did the granddaughter cry?

_____

6 What are the two problems with urban exploration?

_____

3 CRITICAL THINKING **Read the opinions. Which ones are in favour of urban exploration and which are against? Do you agree or disagree? Give reasons.**

1 'Urban exploration is illegal and dangerous. We need to stop people doing it.'

2 'As long as the explorers are careful and respect the main principles, what's the problem?'

3 'We need stricter laws to control it. This isn't a hobby, it's a crime.'

4 Imagine you are an urban explorer. Describe a place that you have explored recently (80–100 words). Explain where it was, what you saw and how you felt.

DEVELOPING Writing

A biography

1 **INPUT** **Look at the photo. What kind of person do you think the woman is? Write four or five words to say what you think.**

Adventurous, _____

_____

ANN BANCROFT

1 Ann Bancroft is an American writer and explorer. She was born in Minnesota and grew up in what she called a family of risk-takers. She became a PE teacher and then a wilderness instructor.

2 In 1986 she got the chance to join an expedition to the North Pole, so she gave up her teaching job and went. After 56 days she became the first woman to get to the North Pole, walking and using a dog sled. Later, she became the first woman ever to get to both the North Pole and the South Pole, crossing the polar ice caps to do so. Then she was the first woman to ski across Greenland.

3 Bancroft often does expeditions with all-women teams. For example, in 1993 she took a group of women on skis to the South Pole. In 2001, she skied across Antarctica with Liv Arnesen.

4 However, she doesn't only go to cold places. In 2015 she took a group – all women, of course – across India, walking along the river Ganges from the Himalaya mountains to the Bay of Bengal, in order to bring attention to the world's water problems. People could follow the expedition online. It was another example of Bancroft's desire to use her expeditions to educate people about the environment.

2 **Read the biography of Ann Bancroft and answer the questions.**

1 What does she say her family was like?

_____

2 What were her first jobs?

_____

3 Name three of her achievements.

_____

4 What is special about most of her expeditions?

_____

5 What did her 2015 expedition aim to do?

_____

3 **ANALYSE** **Label the paragraphs (1–4) with the information (a–d).**

a Something special about her expeditions
b Conclusion / summary of main point of interest about her
c Introduction to the person / background
d Main achievements

4 **PLAN** **Choose a real person (famous, or someone you know) or a fictional character from a book or TV show to write a biography for. The person must explore things or places. Make notes on these things.**

- Do some research about him/her.
- What kind of explorer is this person (someone who actually goes to new places, someone who explored ideas, or someone from the past)?

5 **PRODUCE** **Write your biography (200–250 words). Use your notes from Exercise 4 to help you.**

Write your own checklist.

✓ CHECKLIST

☐ _____
☐ _____
☐ _____
☐ _____

1 🔊 12.01 **Listen and match the photos to the correct person: Bram (B), Rejane (R) or Javi (J).**

 A  B  C

2 🔊 12.01 **Listen again and answer the questions.**

1 What is the Amsterdamse Bos?

_____

2 What is Bram's favourite thing to do when he goes to the Amsterdamse Bos?

_____

3 Where is Rejane's favourite place?

_____

4 Apart for the geographical features she mentions, what else can you see there?

_____

5 Where is Chachapoyas?

_____

6 What is Javi's favourite place to hike to in Chachapoyas?

_____

3 🔊 12.01 **Complete the sentences. Then decide which place they refer to: Amsterdamse Bos (AB), Praia do Sancho (PS) or Chachapoyas (C). Listen again to check.**

1 You can _____ on the tram to get there. ☐

2 There's such a wide variety of geographical features here, including _____ and _____ . ☐

3 The golden sand _____ are stunning and there's a beautiful _____ and some incredible _____ . ☐

4 There's also a climbing park where you can _____ from tree to tree … ☐

5 If I could only _____ , then this would be it. ☐

6 It's a small town hidden in a _____ in the Andes _____ . ☐

PRONUNCIATION
Intrusive /r/ Go to page 121. 🎧

DIALOGUE

1 **Put the sentences in order to make dialogues.**

1 ☐ **Alfie** Well, perhaps you should be a little more open-minded. I tell you what – I'd like to see it again, so why don't you come with me? I'll pay.

☐ **Alfie** We went to see that new film last night. It was really good.

☐ **Alfie** Yes, OK, but a film's more than just one actor, isn't it? Maybe you didn't like those films for other reasons.

☐ **Alfie** Really? Just because you don't like one of the actors?

☐ **Emma** Yes, really. I've seen lots of films with him in and I didn't like any of them.

☐ **Emma** The one with Mark Wahlberg? I don't like him. I don't want to see it.

☐ **Emma** OK, you've persuaded me. But if I don't like it, I'll leave in the middle.

☐ **Emma** Well, maybe – I mean, you could be right. But I'm still not going to see it.

2 ☐ **Grace** Oh, but you should consider it, Billy. All you've got to do is read a book every two weeks. that's not much, is it?

☐ **Grace** Have you heard about the new club at school? The book club?

☐ **Grace** You know, I heard about an app for slow readers – you put it on your phone and it helps you start to read faster. Maybe that would help you. What do you think?

☐ **Grace** Absolutely. You know I love reading and I love talking! Are you going to join?

☐ **Billy** Yeah, I heard about it. Have you joined it?

☐ **Billy** Now that sounds like a great idea. I'll go and look for it now. And then maybe I'll join the club!

☐ **Billy** Well, maybe not for you, but I'm a slow reader – a book a fortnight, that's a lot for me.

☐ **Billy** No, no way. It's really not the kind of thing I'm into, you know.

2 **Choose a situation. Write a dialogue (6–8 lines) between the two people.**

1 There's a school trip to an old city. Julie thinks she doesn't really want to go because she doesn't like old things. Jason tries to persuade her to go because it'll be interesting and there are some great places to eat in the city.

2 Ali is thinking of leaving school next year to get any job he can. He hasn't been doing well at school or in his exams. Sara tries to persuade him to stay another year and get some qualifications, which will help him get a better job when he leaves.

B2 First for Schools

EXAM GUIDE

In Part 2 of the B2 First for Schools Listening Exam, you will hear one long monologue. This may be a talk, a presentation, or part of a radio programme. You will have to complete a short text (consisting of 10 sentences) about the monologue, using the information you hear in the recording. You will hear the exact word(s) you need to complete the gaps. You will hear the recording twice.

Before you listen, it is important to:

- read the title and the whole text, as this will help you to prepare for what you're going to hear.
- think about the type of information, and the types of words you may need to complete the gaps.
- underline the key words.

While you listen, it is important to:

- remember that the questions follow the same order as the recording. If you miss something, move on to the next sentence, and get back to it the second time you listen.
- remember that you should write one, two or three words in each gap.
- focus carefully on the details.
- re-read your completed sentences to make sure they make sense.

1   🔊 12.03   **You will hear a student called Isabella Gill talking about her recent trip to Cuba to study a tiny bird called the bee hummingbird. For questions 1–10, complete the sentences with a word or short phrase.**

The Bee Hummingbird

Isabella was working on a project that was studying bee hummingbird
(1) _____ on the trip.

Isabella says that around **(2)** _____ of bee hummingbirds' habitat has been destroyed on Cuba.

Isabella compares the bee hummingbird to a **(3)** _____ when trying to describe their size.

Isabella was surprised to find out that **(4)** _____ sometimes eat bee hummingbirds.

Isabella uses the word **(5)** _____ to describe how she felt when she spotted her first bee hummingbird.

Isabella says checking the colour of a bird's **(6)** _____ is the best way to tell if it's male or female.

Isabella found out that flowers shaped like **(7)** _____ are the best for bee hummingbirds to feed on.

Isabella says that bee hummingbirds need to eat **(8)** _____ their own body weight of food each day.

Isabella says bee hummingbird babies are fed mainly on very small
(9) _____ by their mothers.

Isabella states that bee hummingbirds use **(10)** _____ to make their nests stronger.

CONSOLIDATION

🎧 LISTENING

1 🔊 12.04 **Listen to the dialogue. Matteo and Nina are talking about an urban explorer. Tick (✓) the places where Matteo has taken photos.**

1 in a train ☐
2 in an underground tunnel ☐
3 at the top of a bridge ☐
4 from a moving car ☐
5 in an empty office building ☐

2 🔊 12.04 **Listen again. Mark the statements T (true) or F (false).**

1 Nina doesn't know what 'urban exploration' is. ☐
2 The photos in the tunnel were taken in the daytime. ☐
3 The explorer took photos at the top of a railway bridge. ☐
4 Nina thought Matteo would be interested in urban exploration. ☐
5 Matteo thinks urban exploration would allow him to do different types of photography. ☐
6 The explorer does his exploring on his own. ☐
7 The explorer uses a fictional name on his website. ☐
8 Matteo decides he still wants to do urban exploration. ☐

🔤 VOCABULARY

3 **Match the sentences.**

1 How often do you see your cousins? ☐
2 So, was the film really exciting? ☐
3 The food was fantastic, wasn't it? ☐
4 How can I help you understand? ☐
5 Hello, can I help you? ☐
6 She's very practical, isn't she? ☐
7 Why shouldn't I swim out there? ☐
8 How come you got wet? ☐

a Yes, it was out of this world.
b Well, give me another example of what you mean.
c Yes, very down to earth.
d Well, there's a dangerous reef just below the surface.
e Oh, only once in a blue moon.
f I got too close to the waterfall.
g Yes. I want to make a complaint.
h Absolutely – it was action-packed.

4 **Circle the correct options.**

1 We've been working all day but we haven't *made / done* much progress.
2 The view from the top of the mountain was *stunning / sentimental*.
3 It was really great news – I was over the *moon / world*.
4 Let's *make / take* advantage of the good weather and go for a walk.
5 Let me *make / give* you some advice.
6 It was really hard to believe – very *far-fetched / down to earth*.
7 Come on, it's easy – it isn't rocket *physics / science*.
8 I need to find a way to *do / make* amends with Charlotte.

Ⓖ GRAMMAR

5 **Rewrite each sentence using the word in capitals. Do not change the word in capitals.**

1 It is possible that they'll come. **MIGHT**
_____

2 He was absent from school. He had a bad cold. **DUE**
_____

3 The earthquake destroyed the house. **BY**
_____

4 I'm 100 percent sure that he will win. **BOUND**
_____

5 It's not possible that you tried your hardest. **CAN'T**
_____

6 It's probable that there will be bad weather at the weekend. **LIKELY**
_____

7 My grandparents gave me some money. **GIVEN**
_____

8 People think that the president is doing a good job. **THOUGHT**
_____

DIALOGUE

6 Complete the dialogue with the phrases in the list. There are two you don't need.

> a shame | dear | don't act
> pity | poor | the consequences
> terrible | vitally important

Dan Have you heard they're planning to build a factory near the coast?

Flora No! How ¹_____ ! It'll spoil the coastline completely.

Dan I know. And I also heard that they're thinking of buying people's houses to make room for it – including my grandmother's house.

Flora ²_____ her!

Dan So ³_____ are going to be pretty bad, I think. If people round here ⁴_____ soon, they'll just go ahead with it. But some people don't seem to care. I tried to talk to some of my friends, but they're not interested.

Flora What ⁵_____ . I think it's ⁶_____ to do something. Come on, let's sit down and get some ideas together.

Dan Great. I knew you'd understand, Flora!

📖 READING

7 Read the article and answer the questions.

1 Why did the writer not watch old films in the past?

_____

2 How long has the writer been a fan of sci-fi films?

_____

3 In *Silent Running* there are six domes. What do they contain?

_____

4 Who helps Lowell in the domes?

_____

5 What order does Lowell decide to disobey?

_____

6 What is the purpose of the fake explosion?

_____

7 How does Lowell try to ensure that the final dome survives?

_____

8 Who remains in the last dome?

_____

🎬 FILMREVIEWS

About   New reviews

An oldie but a goldie – Silent Running

I don't know about you, but I tend to think that films that are 40 or 50 years old aren't going to be all that good – after all, they were mostly made before many of the special-effect techniques that we see today were invented. So for a long time, if I saw that a film was made in, say, 1970 or 1980, I'd decide not to watch it. Now, though, I am beginning to realise that I've been making a mistake, because there are some excellent films out there that might not be technically as good as the ones that are released these days, but that have great acting, storylines and direction. One of these – and here I speak as only a recent convert to science-fiction films – is the 1972 classic *Silent Running*.

It's all set in the future (of course), where all the plants on Earth have become extinct. Some examples of Earth plant life have been put into six huge domes that are like greenhouses and are sent into space, where they are suspended not far from the planet Saturn. The star of the film is Lowell (played by Bruce Dern) who is the botanist in charge of the domes. He's got three people to help him, together with three robots that he nicknames Huey, Dewey and Louie. (As you may recognise, these are named after the three young ducks who are Donald Duck's nephews in cartoon films.)

One day, the people on Earth decide that the domes aren't worth keeping any more, and Lowell and the others are ordered to destroy them with nuclear bombs. After four of the domes have been blown up, Lowell realises he doesn't want the last two to be destroyed – he decides to disobey the order. He goes to his favourite dome and when the other three men come to blow it up, he kills one of them and traps the other two, but as he does this, he hurts his knee very badly.

Then Lowell sets up a fake explosion to make people on Earth think that all the domes have been destroyed. He also gets the robots to do an operation on his knee. After that, he takes the dome on a very dangerous and difficult journey through Saturn's rings. Louie is lost but Lowell and the other two robots get through to the other side. Lowell starts to reprogram the two remaining robots. He teaches them, for example, how to plant trees and how to play card games.

But then a spaceship from Earth arrives to check out what's actually happened. Lowell desperately wants the dome to survive, so he sends it out into space with just Dewey and a watering can on board.

What happens to Lowell? Well, you'll have to watch the film yourself! And it's a great film, so see if you can find it and watch it. I'm sure you won't regret making the effort.

✏️ WRITING

8 Write a paragraph about a science-fiction film you really like or dislike (100–120 words).

PRONUNCIATION

UNIT 1
Diphthongs: alternative spellings

1 **Say the words and write them in the table.**

> allow | although | ate | boil | climb | decide
> enjoy | height | high | hole | how | join
> know | loud | noise | shout | straight
> tiptoe | wait | weight

/eɪ/ rain	/aɪ/ pie	/əʊ/ coat	/aʊ/ out	/ɔɪ/ boy
			allow	

2 🔊 1.01 **Listen, check and repeat.**

UNIT 2
Phrasal verb stress

1 **Tick the sentence in each pair which includes a phrasal verb. Then mark the word you think will be most stressed in each of the underlined phrases for all of the sentences.**

0 What are you going to <u>wear to</u> the party?

   After PE today we were all <u>worn out</u>! ☑

1 They <u>had to pick a</u> colour for their team. ☐
   She <u>picked up</u> French really easily. ☐

2 The cake I made yesterday <u>turned out</u> to be delicious! ☐
   Can you <u>turn and</u> face the board, please? ☐

3 I <u>want to hang</u> a picture on that wall. ☐
   I always <u>hang out with</u> my friends on Saturdays. ☐

4 Sarah's ill; she's <u>going through</u> a difficult time. ☐
   We're <u>going to the</u> city to see a play; would you like to come? ☐

5 I think it's better if we <u>all bring our own</u> food to the party. ☐
   Spring <u>brings about</u> many changes in the countryside. ☐

6 I don't know <u>where to put</u> the papers they've left behind. ☐
   My neighbours make a lot of noise but I just have to <u>put up with</u> it. ☐

> **Remember:** We stress the particle in a phrasal verb more than the verb because it's very important – it changes the meaning of the verb.

2 🔊 2.01 **Listen, check and repeat.**

UNIT 3
Adding emphasis

1 🔊 3.02 **Rewrite the sentences adding *so*, *such*, *do*, *does* or *did*. Listen and check your answers.**

0 Jack McDonald's a good football player!
   Jack McDonald's such a good football player!

1 John gets on well with his parents.
   _____

2 We had a fantastic holiday!
   _____

3 It may not seem like it, but he likes you.
   _____

4 I didn't pass the test – but I studied hard.
   _____

5 What a wonderful day – I love it when the sun's shining!
   _____

2 **Try saying the sentences with and without *so*, *such*, *do*, *does* and *did*. What difference do you notice?**

3 🔊 3.02 **Listen again and repeat the sentences with *so*, *such*, *do*, *does* and *did*.**

UNIT 4
Pronouncing words with *gh*

1   Write the words in the table.

> although | brought | caught | cough | daughter
> enough | fight | ghost | height | high | laugh
> light | straight | thought | tough | through | weigh

gh silent	gh pronounced /f/	gh pronounced /g/
although		

2   🔊 4.01   **Listen, check and repeat.**

3   Match the words in the list that rhyme with words a–l below.

> sport | buy | half | late | off | play | stuff
> taught | toast | you | water | white

a   thought   *sport*
b   laugh   _____
c   enough   _____
d   through   _____
e   ghost   _____
f   high   _____
g   straight   _____
h   height   _____
i   weigh   _____
j   brought   _____
k   daughter   _____
l   cough   _____

4   🔊 4.02   **Listen, check and repeat.**

UNIT 5
The schwa sound

1   Complete the text with the words *to, and, of, for, or, a, the* or *an*.

0   Thank you ___*for*___ calling David's telephone service.
1   This is _____ recorded message.
2   There are no operators free to take your call at _____ moment.
3   Press 1 _____ leave a message.
4   Press 2 if you wish to speak to _____ operator.
5   Please don't shout _____ scream at the operators.
6   Now please hang up _____ make yourself a cup _____ tea.

2   🔊 5.01   **Listen, check and repeat.**

3   Circle the other unstressed words in each sentence which have little meaning and which have the schwa /ə/ sound.

UNIT 6
Linking words with /dʒ/ and /tʃ/

1   Complete the sentences with the words in the list. Circle the words linked with the /dʒ/ sound and underline the words linked with a /tʃ/ sound.

> should | can't | could | did | do
> don't | just | won't | would

0   There's an extra blanket, *should* you need it.
1   You come from Australia, _____ you?
2   How _____ you learn to paint so well?
3   _____ you like a cup of tea and a biscuit?
4   _____ you know how to do a Sudoku?
5   _____ you move out of the way, please? I can't see the TV.
6   You must be tired after your long walk. _____ you sit down?
7   I haven't told anyone my secret – _____ you.
8   You can swim, _____ you?

2   🔊 6.02   **Listen, check and repeat.**

UNIT 7
Intonation: encouraging someone

1 🔊 7.02 **Listen to the sentences, paying particular attention to the underlined phrases. Does the speaker sound interested (I) or uninterested (U)? Write I or U in the box next to each sentence.**

0 Don't <u>let it get you down</u>. People fail their driving test all the time. [U]

1 Try to <u>look on the bright side</u> – if it's raining we can stay in and watch TV. [ ]

2 I know <u>you can do it</u>. You just need a few more lessons. [ ]

3 <u>Don't worry</u> – everything will be fine in the end. [ ]

4 <u>Cheer up</u>. Things will seem better after a good night's sleep. [ ]

5 <u>Hang in there</u>. Your exams will be over soon. [ ]

6 It's <u>not the end of the world</u> – and we've got a day off next week. [ ]

2 **Repeat the sentences trying to sound interested in all of them.**

UNIT 8
Weak forms with conditionals

1 **Circle the contractions *could've*, *should've* and *would've* where they're pronounced *coulda* /ˈkʊdə/, *shoulda* /ˈʃʊdə/ and *woulda* /ˈwʊdə/ without the /v/ sound.**

0 I (would've) come if I'd known Kylie was going to be there.

1 You should've seen the waves at the beach yesterday – they were enormous!

2 Sarah could've passed the test but she didn't study for it.

3 Marley would've asked you to help him if he'd known you were free.

4 We didn't know Jack was in hospital – we would've sent a card if we'd known.

5 I should've eaten breakfast – I'm really hungry now!

6 The accident would've been much worse if they'd been driving faster.

7 You could've told me – you knew it was Dad's birthday yesterday!

Remember: You don't have to say the contractions this way – but hearing them will help you understand native speakers better.

2 🔊 8.01 **Listen, check and repeat.**

UNIT 9
Linking: intrusive /w/ and /j/

1 🔊 9.01 **Listen to the sentences and write /w/ or /j/ above the spaces between the underlined words to indicate which intrusive sound you hear.**

             /j/
0 My parents tell <u>me off</u> all the time. They're always

  /w/
so angry with me!

1 <u>Marie always</u> has a solution to everything.

2 Have <u>you eaten</u> yet? Would you like some <u>tea and</u> biscuits?

3 Do <u>you understand</u> the question? If not, I might <u>be able</u> to help you.

4 I'm <u>so upset</u>! We've lost another match. Why do <u>we always</u> lose?

5 If <u>she ever</u> needs a lift she can come with us. We've got room for <u>two in</u> the back.

6 I don't want to <u>see another</u> film like that. It was <u>too awful</u> for words!

7 <u>I asked</u> Ashley <u>to explain</u> her problem to me.

2 🔊 9.01 **Listen again, check and repeat.**

Remember: You don't have to include the /w/ and /j/ sounds when you speak – but hearing them will help you understand native speakers better.

UNIT 10
Linking: omission of the /h/ sound

1 🔊 10.01 **Listen to the story and cross out the letter *h* when it's silent.**

Hugo was a hairdresser in a hotel. Harry went to him for a haircut.

Hugo spent an hour cutting Harry's hair. The haircut was horrible and Harry wasn't happy.

He decided to be honest and tell Hugo how he felt. He didn't want to pay for his haircut.

Hugo was upset because he liked the haircut and he also wanted his money.

In the end, Harry paid him half.

2 🔊 10.01 **Listen again and check your answers.**

3 **There are two words where the letter *h* is always silent at the beginning. What are they?**

UNIT 11
Stress on modal verbs for speculation

1 🔊 11.01 **Listen to the pairs of sentences and decide when the speaker thinks it is likely (L) or unlikely (U) that the event will happen or is true. Write 'L' or 'U' in the boxes.**

0 A   I just watched a TV show that said aliens might have visited Earth. [U]

  B   I just watched a TV show that said aliens might have visited Earth. [L]

1 A   I invited Sally and Jack to our party. They said they might come. [ ]

  B   I invited Sally and Jack to our party. They said they might come. [ ]

2 A   They say she may win an Oscar for her role in that film. [ ]

  B   They say she may win an Oscar for her role in that film. [ ]

3 A   Do you want to try that new restaurant? It could be really good. [ ]

  B   Do you want to try that new restaurant? It could be really good. [ ]

4 A   Someone told me that Elvis might still be alive. [ ]

  B   Someone told me that Elvis might still be alive. [ ]

5 A   I might become an author when I'm older. [ ]

  B   I might become an author when I'm older. [ ]

2 🔊 11.01 **Listen again, check and repeat the sentences where the speaker thinks it's likely (L).**

3 🔊 11.01 **Listen again, check and repeat the sentences where the speaker thinks it's unlikely (U).**

UNIT 12
Linking: intrusive /r/

1 **Read the sentences. Each one contains the intrusive /r/ sound which often links two words that start and end with vowel sounds. Write *r* above the spaces where you think this sound appears. There is one in each sentence.**

0   Join us on ‸ʳ our adventure to faraway places!

1   I don't know why they're angry with us. We didn't do anything wrong!

2   Some animals are finding it harder and harder to live on our planet.

3   From her accent I'd say Julie is French.

4   We're flying into Atlanta airport on our trip to the USA.

5   It's another awful day – I wish it wasn't raining again!

6   I'd like to go to Australia and America when I'm older.

7   Hannah always leaves her homework until the last minute.

2 🔊 12.02 **Listen, check and repeat.**

> **Remember:** You don't have to include the /r/ sounds when you speak – but hearing it will help you understand native speakers better.

GRAMMAR REFERENCE

UNIT 1
Verb patterns: *to* + infinitive or gerund

1 **When a verb is followed by another verb, the second verb is either in the gerund form (*-ing*) or it is an infinitive with *to*.**

2 **These verbs are followed by a gerund: *imagine, feel like, suggest, practise, miss, can't stand, enjoy, detest,* and *don't mind*.**

   *I **enjoy cooking** but I **can't stand washing** the dishes.*

3 **These verbs are followed by an infinitive with *to*: *decide, refuse, hope, promise, ask, expect, afford, offer* and *choose*.**

   *I can't **afford to buy** a new smart phone.*

4 **These verbs can be followed by either form with no difference in meaning: *begin, start, continue*.**

   *We **started walking** / **to walk** towards the town.*
   *It **continued raining** / **to rain** until late afternoon.*

Verbs + gerund and *to* + infinitive with different meanings

The verbs *remember, try, stop, regret, forget* can be followed by either form (gerund or infinitive) but with a difference in meaning. The difference relates to time: which action came first (1) and which came second (2). In general, verb + gerund looks back, and verb + infinitive looks forward.

remember

*I **remember going** there last year. (I went last year (1) and some time later, I remembered (2))*
*I **remembered to go** to the supermarket. (First I remembered (1) and then I went (2))*

forget

*I'll never **forget meeting** you. (First I met you (1) and now I won't forget (2))*
*Don't **forget to meet** me at the cinema. (First don't forget (1) and then meet me at the cinema (2))*

stop

*We **stopped eating** and left the café. (First we ate (1) and then we stopped (2))*
*We **stopped to eat** our sandwiches. (First we stopped (1) and then we ate (2))*

try

*I **tried taking** the medicine but I still felt ill. (I felt ill. I took the medicine. After the medicine, I didn't feel better.)*
*I **tried to take** the medicine but I couldn't swallow it. (= I wanted to take the medicine, but I was unsuccessful.)*

regret

*I really **regret telling** him what happened. (First I told him what happened (1) I am sorry that I told him (2))*
*I **regret to tell** you that you failed the exam. (You failed (1) and I'm sorry to have to tell you this (2))*

UNIT 2
Relative clauses (review)

1 **A defining relative clause identifies the thing, person, place or possession that we are talking about. We do not use a comma in these clauses.**

   *The woman **who** gives the lectures is very intelligent. (= There is only one woman who gives the lectures.)*
   *The city **where** I grew up is a great place. (= I am talking about the only city where I grew up.)*

2 **A non-defining relative clause gives additional information about the thing, person, place or possession we are talking about. This information is between commas.**

   *The woman, **who** gives the lectures, is very intelligent. (= I am talking about an intelligent woman and adding the non-essential information that she gives lectures.)*
   *The city, **where** I grew up, is a great place. (= I am talking about a city that's a great place, and adding that it is where I grew up.)*

which to refer to a whole clause

When we want to refer back to a clause or an idea, we use the relative pronoun *which* (not *that* or *what*)

*He had to go out and find a job, **which** wasn't easy.*
*This phone is very good, **which** is why it's so popular.*

Omitting relative pronouns and reduced relative clauses

1 **When the relative pronouns *that / which / who* are the object of the following clause, they can be omitted. They can't be omitted when they are the subject of the following clause.**

   *He's the man (**that**) I told you about.*
   *He's the boy **who** sold me this watch.*

2   When the relative pronoun is followed by the verb *be*, we can leave out both the relative pronoun and the verb *be*. This is called a 'reduced relative clause'.

*Their house, (**which was**) built only last year, was completely destroyed by the tornado.*
*The people (**who are**) running the company are not doing their job properly.*

UNIT 3
Quantifiers

1   **Quantifiers are words that we use to say how many or how much of a noun. Frequent quantifiers are:**

none, hardly any, a few / a little, (not) many / much, some, several, most, a lot / lots, loads, all

2   **The quantifiers *a few* / (*not*) *many* / *several* are only used with countable nouns. The quantifiers *a little* / (*not*) *much* are only used with uncountable nouns.**

*I've been to **a few / many / several** rock **concerts**.*
*They took **a little food** on the trip.*
*They didn't take **much food** on the trip.*

3   **Some quantifiers always need the word *of* before the noun or pronoun they refer to:**

***None of** the books were cheap.*
***A lot of** people think that way.*

4   **All the quantifiers need the word *of* when they are followed by a pronoun:**

*Hardly any films are made here, and **hardly any of them** are good.*
*There is some food in the fridge, but **some of it** is quite old.*

5   **The word *none* (*of*) is grammatically singular but many people use a plural verb after it.**

*I've got lots of friends, but **none of** them **are** musicians.*

so and *such* (review)

1   **We use the words *so* and *such* to emphasise what we are saying:**

*This food is **so** delicious!   She's **such** a good writer.*

2   **We use *so* + adjective. We use *such* (+ adjective) + noun (or pronoun).**

*The weather's **so** good.   It's **such** a wonderful day.*

3   **We can follow these phrases with a *that* clause, to show consequences.**

*The weather was so good **that** we went for a walk.*
*It was such good weather **that** we went for a walk.*

do and *did* for emphasis

We can use the auxiliary verb *do* / *does* (or *did* in the past) to emphasise the verb.

*I **did like** the food! I just wasn't very hungry.*
*We didn't have time to go to the museum, but we **did go** to the park.*

UNIT 4
be / *get used to* (doing) vs. *used to* (do)

1   **When we want to talk about something being normal or familiar, we can use the expression *be used to*.**

*It's cold where I live, so I'**m used to wearing** a lot of warm clothes.*

2   **We use *get used to* to refer to the process of something becoming normal or familiar.**

*It took him a while to **get used to eating** dinner early.*

3   **These expressions are followed by a noun or the gerund (-*ing*) form of a verb.**

*I'm not really **used to** spicy **food**.*
*They've **got used** to **living** in a small apartment.*

4   **These expressions are not the same as *used to*, which refers to past habits or states which are no longer true and is followed by an infinitive without *to*.**

*I **used to love** their music, but now I never listen to it.*

Adverbs and adverbial phrases

Adverbs qualify verbs. They can qualify verbs in different ways, for example:

Adverbs of manner (*how*)	He walked **quickly**.
Adverbs of time (*when*)	We got there **late**.
Adverbs of place (*where*)	Sign **here**, please.
Adverbs of probability	You **probably** think I'm crazy!
Adverbs of opinion	It's **surprisingly** quiet in here.

We can also use adverbial phrases to describe a verb and to say how an action is/was performed.

One structure for adverbial phrases is *with* + noun.

*When I told her, she reacted **with surprise**.*

Another structure for adverbial phrases is *in a(n)* + adjective + *way*.

*Our teacher explains things **in a fun way**.*

Adverbial phrases are often used when an adjective (e.g. *friendly, difficult, interesting, fun*) has no adverb form.

UNIT 5
Obligation, permission and prohibition (review)

1   **We can talk about obligation and necessity by using *must, have to* and *(be) supposed to*.**

    *You **must** get there before eight o'clock. (= This is an obligation imposed by the speaker.)*
    *We **have to** finish our projects by Friday. (= This is an obligation imposed by someone else.)*
    *We**'re supposed to** switch off our phones in lessons.* (= This is the rule, but we don't always follow it.)

2   **We can talk about no obligation or no necessity by using *don't have to* and *don't need to*.**

    *You **don't have to** eat this if you don't want to.*
    *We **didn't need to** buy tickets – my dad gave us some.*

3   **We can say something is (or isn't) a good idea by using *should(n't)*.**

    *You **should** leave now if you don't want to miss your bus.*
    *I **shouldn't** eat any more or I'll feel sick.*

4   **We can talk about permission using *let* or *be allowed to*. *Let* is active voice, while *be allowed to* is passive voice.**

    *The school **lets** us use the tennis courts at the weekend.*
    *We're **allowed to** use the tennis courts at the weekend.*

5   **We can talk about prohibition using *(not) be allowed to* or *don't/doesn't let*. When we don't know, or don't want to say who it is that prohibits something, we use 'they'.**

    *Cyclists **are not allowed to** leave their bikes here.*
    ***They don't let** cyclists leave their bikes here.*

Necessity: *(didn't) need to / needn't have*

We use *didn't need to* and *needn't have* to talk about the past necessity of actions. There is a small but important difference between the structures.

1   ***didn't need to* usually suggests that we didn't do something because it wasn't necessary.**

    *I **didn't need to** go to the doctor. (I didn't go.)*

2   ***needn't have* means that we did something but actually it wasn't necessary.**

    *We **needn't have** cooked all this food – only four people turned up at the party. (We cooked a lot of food but it wasn't necessary.)*

Ability in the past: *could, was / were able to, managed to, succeeded in doing*

1   **When we talk about ability in the past, we can use *could/couldn't, managed to, was/were able to* or *succeeded (in doing)*. However, there are differences between them.**

2   **We use *could / couldn't* to talk about general ability in the past.**

    *My brother **couldn't ride** a bike until he was twelve.*
    *I **could do** maths in my head when I was a kid.*

3   **When we want to talk about <u>no</u> ability on a specific occasion in the past, we have three possibilities:**

    *I listened, but I **couldn't hear** anything.*
    *I worked hard, but I **didn't manage to finish** everything.*
    *I hurt my leg and I **wasn't able to walk** for two weeks.*

4   **But, when we want to talk about ability on a specific occasion in the past, we don't use *could*:**

    *The wall was very high but we **managed to climb** over it. (NOT: we ~~could climb~~ over it.)*
    *Because we bought our tickets a long time in advance, we **were able to get** them quite cheaply. (NOT: we ~~could get~~ them …)*

5   **We use *succeeded (in doing)* to emphasise that something was difficult in the past but we were able to do it.**

    *I had to wait for hours, but I **succeeded in getting** tickets.*

UNIT 6
Comparatives

1   **We can intensify a comparison (make it stronger) using *a lot / far / much* + comparative adjective.**

    *Use a calculator – it's **far easier** that way.*
    *Let's take a taxi, it's **much quicker**.*
    *It's **a lot more difficult** than I thought.*

2   **Comparisons with *as … as* can be made stronger with *not nearly* or *nowhere near*.**

    *He isn't **nearly as clever as** his sister. (His sister is much cleverer than him.)*
    *The film is **nowhere near as good as** the book. (The book is far better than the film.)*

3   **We can use *just* with *as … as* to emphasise how similar two things are.**

    *Our team is **just as good as** yours. (The two teams are really equally good.)*

4   We can use comparative *and* comparative with short adjectives or *more and more* + adjective with longer adjectives to show how comparisons become stronger over time.

*My little sister's getting **bigger and bigger** every day.*
*Train tickets are getting **more and more expensive.***

5   We can use *the* + comparative (+ clause), *the* + comparative (+ clause) with short adjectives, or *the more* ... adjective (+ clause), *the more* ... adjective (+ clause) with longer adjectives, to show how two events affect each other.

The longer I sat there, the more uncomfortable I became.
The older people are, the more interesting they are.

Linkers of contrast

1   The linkers *although* and *even though* are followed by a clause. They can be used at the beginning of a sentence, or before the second clause.

*I passed my driving test, **although / even though** I made some mistakes.*
***Although / Even though** I made some mistakes in my driving test, I passed.*

2   The linkers *despite* and *in spite of* are followed by a noun phrase or a gerund. They can be used at the beginning of a sentence, or before the second clause.

*I passed my driving test, **despite / in spite of** (making) some mistakes.*
***Despite** (making) some mistakes in my driving test, I passed.*

3   The linkers *however* and *nevertheless* come at the beginning of a sentence and introduce a contrast with what was said in the previous sentence.

*I made some mistakes in my driving test. **However / Nevertheless**, I passed.*

UNIT 7
Ways of referring to the future (review)

Some common ways to refer to the future include:

1   *be going to* for plans, intentions and evidence-based predictions

I'm going to visit my grandparents tomorrow.

2   *will* for future facts, spontaneous decisions and offers, and feeling-based predictions

*Technology **will develop** a lot in the next twenty years.*

3   the present continuous for arrangements

*We're **taking** our cat to the vet this afternoon.*

4   the present simple for events that are part of a timetable, and after time expressions like *when, before, after, until,* and *as soon as*

*I'll meet you when you **arrive** tomorrow.*

Future continuous and future perfect

1   The future continuous is formed by *will + be + -ing* form of the verb.

2   We use the future continuous tense to talk about an action that will be in progress at a specified future time.

*When I'm 25, I'll **be living** in another country.*

3   The future perfect tense is formed by *will + have +* the past participle of the verb.

4   We use the future perfect tense to talk about an action that we think will be completed by a specified future time.

*By 2025, the population **will have grown** enormously.*

UNIT 8
Conditionals (review)

1   We use the zero conditional to talk about a condition and its consequence that are always true.

*If I **go** running, I always **feel** better.*

2   We use the first conditional to talk about a condition and its possible future consequence.

*If you **make** a list, you'll **remember** what you need.*

3   We use the second conditional to talk about a hypothetical situation in the present.

*If I **had** more time, I'd **take up** the guitar.*

4   We use the third conditional to talk about an imaginary situation in the past and its consequence in the past which is impossible to change.

*If we **had left** earlier, we **wouldn't have been** late.*

Mixed conditionals

Conditional sentences don't always follow the four patterns described above. It's possible to mix second and third conditionals.

1   If we want to talk about an imaginary / unreal past action and its present consequence, then the *if* clause follows the pattern of a third conditional and the consequence clause follows the pattern of a second conditional.

*If I'd **paid** more attention in class, I'd **know** how to do this exercise. (I didn't pay attention. I don't know how to do this exercise.)*

2   If we want to talk about how a hypothetical or imaginary present could or would change the past, then the *if* clause follows the pattern of a second conditional and the consequence clause follows the pattern of a third conditional.

*If I **had** more self-confidence, I **would have gone** and talked to him. (I didn't go and talk to him, because I don't have much self-confidence.)*

UNIT 9
I wish and *if only*

1   We can use *I wish* or *if only* to talk about how we would like things to be different now or in the future. The verb that follows *I wish / if only* is in the past simple tense.

*I wish I **knew** her name. (I don't know her name and I'm sorry about that.)*

*If only I **could** stay in bed a bit longer. (I can't stay in bed longer, but I want to!)*

2   We can also use *I wish* or *if only* to talk about regrets we have about the past. In this case, the verb that follows *I wish / if only* is in the past perfect tense.

*I wish you**'d told** me about it before.*

*If only I **hadn't missed** that penalty.*

I would prefer to / it if; It's time; *I'd rather / sooner*

1   To talk about our own preferences, we can use *I'd prefer + to* infinitive, or we can use *I'd rather / I'd sooner* + base form. *I'd rather* is far more common than *I'd sooner*.

*I**'d prefer to stay** home tonight.*

*I**'d rather / I'd sooner have** fish than chicken for dinner.*

2   To say what we would like another person to do, we can use *I'd rather / I'd sooner* + subject + past simple tense, or we can use *I'd prefer it if* + subject + past simple tense.

*I'd rather **you phoned** me tomorrow, if that's OK.*

*I'd prefer it if **my friends didn't make** fun of me.*

3   We can use *It's time* + subject + past simple to say that we think someone should do something (and to suggest that it should be done immediately).

*It's time **we left**. (We should leave now.)*

UNIT 10
Reported speech (review)

1   When we report what someone said, there is often a change in verb tense between the direct speech and the reported speech.

*'Someone's **eaten** all the food!' he said.* → *He said someone **had eaten** all the food.*

*'I **can't** do this,' he said.* → *He said he **couldn't** do it.*

2   If the information in the direct speech is still true, we don't necessarily need to change the verb tense.

'He's ill,' she told me → *She told me he's ill.*

Reported questions and requests

1   When we report a *yes/no* question, we use *if* or *whether* and normal word order (subject + verb).

'Do you know this song?' → *She asked me if I **knew** the song. (NOT: She asked me did I know …)*

2   When we report *wh-* questions, we use the same question word and normal word order (subject + verb).

'Where did they go?' → *He asked me **where they'd gone**. (NOT: He asked me where did they go)*

3   When we report a request or order, we use *asked* + person + *to* + infinitive

'Please help me.' → *He **asked me to help** him.*

Verb patterns

We can use many verbs to report what people said. They tell us what kind of thing was said (e.g. a demand, an apology, etc.). There are different patterns that follow the verbs.

The most frequent patterns are:

1   + [person] + infinitive, e.g. *tell / ask / warn / order / advise / persuade*

*They asked **us to leave**.*

2   + *to* + infinitive OR + *that* clause, e.g. *agree*

*He agreed **to go**.*

*He agreed **that** it was a bad idea.*

3   + gerund OR + *that* clause, e.g. *admit / regret / deny / suggest*

*They suggested **walking**.*

*They admitted **that** it was a good thing to do.*

4   + person + *of* + gerund, e.g. *accuse*

*He accused **me of taking** his things without asking.*

UNIT 11
Speculating (past, present and future)

We often use the modal verbs *might* / *may* / *could* / *must* / *can't* to speculate about the present, the past or the future.

1 **We use *might* / *may* / *could* to talk about a possibility.**

   *She **might** / **may** / **could** be Mexican.*

2 **We use *must* when we want to say that we are certain, based on evidence.**

   *You're going swimming in the sea in winter? You **must** be crazy!*

3 **We use *can't* when we believe something is impossible, based on evidence.**

   *There's no one in that restaurant – it **can't** be very good.*

4 **When we speculate about the past, we use the modal verb + *have* + past participle.**

   *Everyone is talking about the film last night – it **must have been** very good.*

   *I'm surprised John wasn't at the party – he was really looking forward to it. He **must have been** sick.*

5 **We can also use *be* + *bound to* / *certain to* / *likely to* to speculate about present and future events. The expression *be likely to* is not as sure as *be bound to* / *be certain to*.**

   *Ask Jo, she's really smart, so she's **bound to** know.*

   *The weather forecast says it's **likely to** rain later today.*

Cause and effect linkers

We use the linkers *due to* / *as a result of* / *because of* / *consequently* to link actions and their consequences.

1 **We use *because of* / *due to* / *as a result of* before the reason for an action or event. These phrases can come at the beginning of a sentence, or in the middle. They are usually followed by a noun or noun phrase.**

   *The government changed its mind **because of** / **due to** / **as a result of** pressure from the population.*

   ***Because of** / **Due to** / **As a result of** pressure from the population, the government changed its mind.*

2 **The word *consequently* introduces the result of a previous idea. It is usually used at the beginning of a new sentence.**

   *Sales of the new car were very low. **Consequently**, the company lowered the price for a few weeks.*

UNIT 12
Passive report structures

1 **We use passive report structures when we want to report information and the agent is not important.**

   *The Amazon rainforest **is known to be** the largest forest in the world. (It is not important to say who thinks this.)*

2 **We mostly use passive report structures with verbs like *say*, *think*, *believe*, *know* and *consider*.**

3 **If we use a passive report structure to talk about beliefs or knowledge in the present, we use *be* + past participle of the reporting verb + infinitive.**

   *Really strange creatures **are thought to exist** in the deep oceans.*

   *She **is considered to be** a real expert on wildlife.*

4 **If we use a passive report structure to talk about beliefs or knowledge in the past, we use *be* + past participle of the reporting verb + *to* + present perfect infinitive.**

   *Dinosaurs **are thought to have disappeared** because of a major disaster on Earth. (They no longer exist.)*

   *They **are known to have had** very small brains.*

5 **Passive report structures are quite formal and are commonly used in news reports.**

The passive: verbs with two objects

1 **Some verbs (like *give*, *offer*, *ask*, *promise*, *read*, *show*, *write*, etc.) have two possible passive forms. This is because these verbs can be followed by two objects – a person and a thing.**

2 **The two possible active forms are:**

   a) verb + indirect object + direct object: *Someone gave me a present.*

   b) verb + direct object + indirect object: *Someone gave a present to me.*

3 **The two possible passive constructions are:**

   a) *I was given a present.* (The person is the subject of the sentence.)

   b) *A present was given to me.* (The thing is the subject of the sentence.)

4 **It is more usual to have the person as the subject of the passive construction (as in 3a) not the thing (as in 3b).**

   The kids were shown a film is more likely than *A film was shown to the kids.*

IRREGULAR VERBS

Base form	Past simple	Past participle
be	was / were	been
bear	bore	borne
beat	beat	beaten
become	became	become
begin	began	begun
bend	bent	bent
bet	bet	bet
bite	bit	bitten
blow	blew	blown
break	broke	broken
breed	bred	bred
bring	brought	brought
broadcast	broadcast	broadcast
build	built	built
burn	burned / burnt	burned / burnt
buy	bought	bought
can	could	–
catch	caught	caught
choose	chose	chosen
come	came	come
cost	cost	cost
cut	cut	cut
deal	dealt	dealt
dive	dived	dived
do	did	done
draw	drew	drawn
dream	dreamed / dreamt	dreamed / dreamt
drink	drank	drunk
drive	drove	driven
eat	ate	eaten
fall	fell	fallen
feed	fed	fed
feel	felt	felt
fight	fought	fought
find	found	found
flee	fled	fled
fly	flew	flown
forbid	forbade	forbidden
forget	forgot	forgotten
forgive	forgave	forgiven
freeze	froze	frozen
get	got	got
give	gave	given
go	went	gone
grow	grew	grown
hang	hung	hung
have	had	had
hear	heard	heard
hide	hid	hidden
hit	hit	hit
hold	held	held
hurt	hurt	hurt
keep	kept	kept
know	knew	known
lay	laid	laid
lead	led	led
learn	learned / learnt	learned / learnt
leave	left	left

Base form	Past simple	Past participle
lend	lent	lent
let	let	let
lie	lay	lain
light	lit	lit
lose	lost	lost
make	made	made
mean	meant	meant
meet	met	met
misunderstand	misunderstood	misunderstood
overcome	overcame	overcome
pay	paid	paid
put	put	put
quit	quit	quit
read /riːd/	read /red/	read /red/
ride	rode	ridden
ring	rang	rung
rise	rose	risen
run	ran	run
say	said	said
see	saw	seen
seek	sought	sought
sell	sold	sold
send	sent	sent
set	set	set
shake	shook	shaken
shine	shone	shone
shoot	shot	shot
show	showed	shown
shut	shut	shut
sing	sang	sung
sink	sank	sunk
sit	sat	sat
sleep	slept	slept
speak	spoke	spoken
speed	sped	sped
spend	spent	spent
spill	spilled / spilt	spilled / spilt
split	split	split
spread	spread	spread
stand	stood	stood
steal	stole	stolen
stick	stuck	stuck
strike	struck	struck
swear	swore	sworn
sweep	swept	swept
swim	swam	swum
swing	swung	swung
take	took	taken
teach	taught	taught
tear	tore	torn
tell	told	told
think	thought	thought
throw	threw	thrown
understand	understood	understood
wake	woke	woken
wear	wore	worn
win	won	won
write	wrote	written